YOUR FUTURE IN TRANSLATING AND INTERPRETING

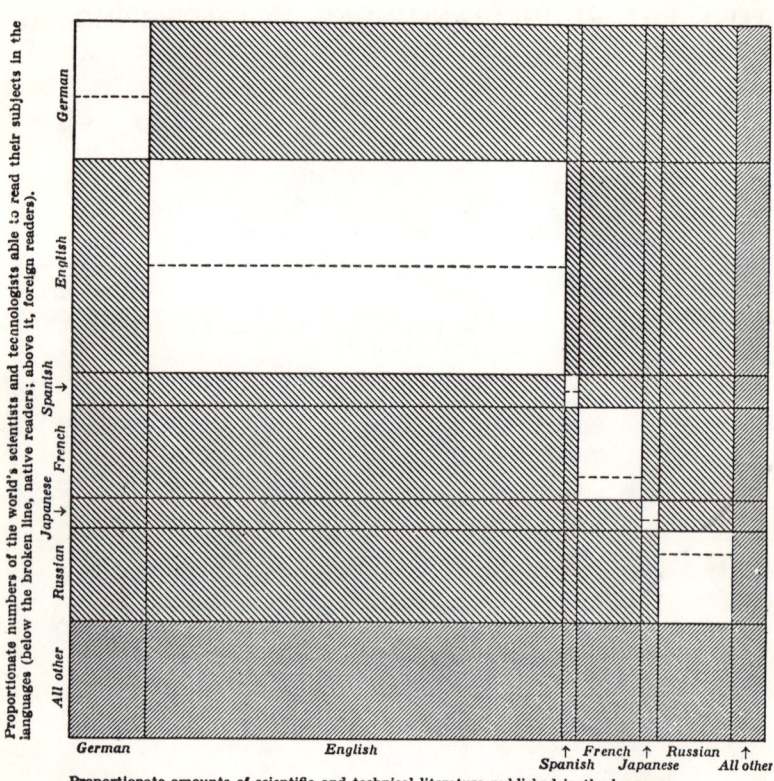

Representative proportions of publications and of readers in six principal languages (from Scientific and Technical Translating).

YOUR FUTURE IN TRANSLATING AND INTERPRETING

by J. F. HENDRY

RICHARDS ROSEN PRESS, INC., NEW YORK 10010

LIBRARY
CENTRAL PIEDMONT COMMUNITY COLLEGE
P. O. BOX 4009
CHARLOTTE, N. C. 28204

Standard Book Number: 8239-0086-x
Library of Congress Catalog Card Number: 69-19137
Dewey Decimal Classification: 371.42

Published 1969 by Richards Rosen Press, Inc.
29 East 21st Street, New York City, N.Y. 10010

Copyright 1969 by J. F. Hendry

All rights reserved. No part of this book may be reproduced
in any form without written permission from
the publisher, except by a reviewer.

Revised Edition

Manufactured in the United States of America

About the Author

J. F. Hendry writes of the field of translating and interpreting from a background of study and work in languages that dates from his university days. Born in Glasgow, Scotland, he attended the University of Glasgow, where he received an M.A. with honors in Russian and French, and later studied at the University of London, England, where he obtained a Certificate of Distinction in German, the equivalent of a B.A. with honors. After service with the British Army in World War II, he worked as Translator and Interpreter with the Allied Secretariat, Allied Commission for Austria, and later with the British Embassy in Vienna.

Following a period of language-teaching, he worked as translator with the International Atomic Energy Agency in Vienna and later with the International Labour Office in Geneva, Switzerland. During these years he attended many conferences, as interpreter, translator, or précis writer. He was a member of the United Nations Mission to Rwanda and Burundi in 1962; attended the meeting of the Council of Europe in Strasbourg in 1963; and was for a time attached to the office of the Common Market, in Brussels, Belgium.

In 1966 Professor Hendry was appointed chairman of the Department of Modern Languages at Laurentian University, Sudbury, Ontario, Canada. There he was instrumental in founding the School of Translators and Interpreters, the first school of its kind in Canada and one of the first in North America. His special extracurricular interest is in semiotics, the new science that deals with signs and symbols and their function in language.

Professor Hendry is a member of the Institute of Linguists and a member of the Canadian Association of Slavists, the Canadian Linguistic Association, the International Association of Conference Translators and Interpreters, and collaborator with the International Federation of Translators.

Acknowledgments

Acknowledgments are due to the following organizations for permission to reproduce the illustrations and photographs in these pages: UNESCO (Paris); United Nations (New York); Laurentian University, Sudbury, Ontario, Canada; and The Peace Corps, Washington, D.C.

Acknowledgments are also due to Dr. Stefan Horn, and the School of Languages and Linguistics, Georgetown University, Washington, D.C.

"Speech is civilization itself. The word, even the most contradictory word preserves contact—it is silence which isolates."
>(Thomas Mann: THE MAGIC MOUNTAIN, Chapter 6.)

"There is more ado to interpret interpretation than to interpret the things and more books upon books than upon all other subjects; we do nothing but comment upon one another."
>(Montaigne: ESSAYS, Book III, Chapter 13, OF EXPERIENCE).

Contents

Chapter
I. The Job—Background—Attitudes and Qualifications ... 13
II. The Job—What It Is All About—How to Do It ... 22
III. The Nature of Language—Speaking and Writing—Some Qualitative Aspects of Translation and Interpretation ... 35
IV. The Main Field and the People in It—Précis Writing—The Communication Field ... 50
V. Related Fields and People in Them—"Anything That Talks"—Public Relations ... 64
VI. Job Training and Where to Get It ... 71
VII. How to Get a Job—Conditions to Expect—A Sample Contract ... 81
VIII. Job Satisfaction—Some Perquisites—Travel—Salaries and Allowances ... 94
IX. Health and Security—Retirement and Pension—Currency and Other Hints ... 99
X. How to Make a Self-Evaluation—Opportunities for Women—The Best of Careers ... 105

Appendix
A. Universities and Colleges Offering Degrees in Translation or Courses in Linguistics, With or Without Translation ... 112
B. Publications and Specialized Dictionaries ... 116
C. Reading List ... 122
D. Professional and Other Societies ... 126
E. Interested Firms and Institutions That Are in the Profession ... 128

CHAPTER I

The Job—Background—Attitudes and Qualifications

The rapid growth in the past decade of foreign travel, mass communications, and many new nations has made people in every country aware of their differences, including language differences. It has also made them aware of the vital need to overcome these differences by promoting world understanding.

It is not surprising, therefore, that many new careers should have opened up that attempt to grapple with this new requirement in the world. Among these, none, surely, is more vital than that of the translator or interpreter, whose services are in daily demand in all parts of the globe.

Not everyone, of course, is either interested in, or equipped for, such a career; yet, at some time or other, we all need to do a bit of both translating and interpreting on our own. Some acquaintance with the applicable qualities and techniques is thus of general interest.

Let us see what is involved.

If I were asked to name the one characteristic, above all, that the profession demands, I would venture to say "independence"; not financial independence, naturally, but independence of spirit. As Bacon said: "Travel maketh a full man," and we come to know ourselves best by mingling with others, especially strangers.

Without this independence, enterprise and initiative are scarcely possible; yet these are also important qualities in the translator or interpreter.

We are all aware of the type of individual who cannot go from New York to Cleveland by Greyhound bus without a good deal of fuss and assistance. Many such people may be extremely intelligent—and even acquainted with one or two languages.

Nevertheless, they are not qualified to become translators or interpreters, because their interests are more personal and domestic than social. The fact that they do not find it easy to *adapt* is what causes them to make something of a fuss when they travel. Indeed, it is something of a miracle that they manage to get about as well as they do.

This provides us with one clue, then, as to the type of person whom we are seeking. You've guessed it. We are looking for the type of person who *can* travel from New York to Cleveland, and to Mexico City too, if need be, with the *minimum* of fuss; and one who even helps others to get about, because he or she is interested in the outside world, and is prepared to make the necessary adjustment.

Deeper still, perhaps, is a tendency on the part of the person we are looking for to try and bring people together in friendly relations. It is possible to exaggerate this tendency, but in my own experience the translator or interpreter does have the feeling that he is a link—a human bridge, so to speak—between different mentalities and even social systems.

Paradoxically, it is this independence of spirit that makes possible the adaptation to and exploration of new ideas and new territories that are necessary in the profession.

Successful candidates for this career, then, will usually be good listeners, lively and aware of their surroundings, with an outgoing, or what used to be called, not very aptly, an "extrovert" personality. They will have a natural bent for communication, and perhaps, though not necessarily, the "gift of gab."

This brings us to the next desirable quality, an interest in one's *own* (native) language! Too often, knowledge of a foreign language is taken for granted by employers, as though it were a *sine qua non*. The ability to translate into good English, on the other hand, strangely enough, is often considered as proof that one knows the foreign language, since obviously one can translate from it! Good English, therefore, in practice is the final piece of convincing evidence that a translator knows what he is talking about, and that he has really understood "the message."

In this connection a distinction must be made between the work of the translator and that of the interpreter. These professions are too often confused, even by those who should know

BACKGROUND—ATTITUDES AND QUALIFICATIONS 15

better. It is frequently assumed that there is no difference, that a translator can also interpret, or an interpreter translate. This is not always the case, by any means.

Worse still, the terms are used interchangeably, as though they meant the same thing. They do not.

In the United Nations and its agencies, as well as in most large business organizations, these two careers are kept quite distinct; and they have, in fact, their own separate professional associations, in most cases.

The interpreter, of course, is the one who does the talking. He appears on the stage in person.

The translator does the writing. He is confined to the back room. We may call the interpreter the glamour boy, or girl: the one who sits, wearing earphones very becomingly, in the interpreter's booth at international conferences. When he, or she, translates verbally what the speaker in the foreign language is saying, *as he is saying it,* this is termed *simultaneous* interpretation. When he waits until the speaker has finished, and then translates verbally, this is *consecutive* interpretation. Both of these techniques demand special gifts, the one of quickness and fluency, the other of retentive memory.

Accuracy here is not as important as speed. The interpreter may make a mistake, which can be passed over. The translator, never.

The interpreting of a foreign language into the "target"* language (English in the case of English speakers) requires a perfect ear, immediate understanding of the foreign phrase or idiom, and ability to find the appropriate English counterpart *at once.*

Any hesitation is fatal and leads to distrust and suspicion of an interpreter's abilities. Better to risk error, unless great issues are at stake, and fall back on the generosity of the audience, which is always considerable.

Many amusing stories are told of such errors, and even of wrong attitudes at a conference. An interpreter should try primarily to establish some form of friendly contact with his audience. After the war, a Soviet interpreter at an important four-

---

* The "target" language is the language *into which* the interpreter or translator translates; the "source" language is the language of the text from which he must translate.

power meeting puzzled U.S. and British generals considerably when he announced Soviet agreement to a Western proposal because, although his own General was smiling in friendly fashion, he himself was fiercely scowling! Perhaps it had become a habit.

In consecutive interpretation, attitude can be important, because listeners tend to try and read the interpreter's expression, as well as that of the original speaker, to see what lies behind the actual words. Empathy, or the art of feeling out one's audience, is a great help here in establishing a friendly rapport to begin with.

Whereas the interpreter is the glamour boy or girl, the translator, on the other hand, is the backroom boy. Upon him depend conference records and their accuracy. No mistakes are allowed. The translator also works under a supervisor, whose comments can be extremely scathing should he find serious errors in a translation when he reviews it. True, a translator need not face a battery of faces; the tension of conferences, which can be quite nerve-wracking in these times; the split-second decision; or the ordeal of public speaking. He does his work in peace and quiet. He will probably be able to take as much time as he likes, within reason. On the other hand, he will often be required to reproduce the minutes of a conference, filling in the gaps in tape recordings with the written statements of foreign speakers; or even producing the whole of the official minutes from tape recordings that are a mass of—yes—ill-digested verbiage!

Whereas the interpreter does his job if he repeats verbatim what a foreign speaker *has said,* the translator is expected to translate what he *meant,* and in the case of minutes, even what he did *not* say, but *should* have said! This, of course, calls for a good deal of tact and patience, particularly when his work is rarely rewarded with a word of thanks, unlike that of his glamorous counterpart, who is often treated like a film star.

The interpreter, then, will be a person whose social "bump" is well developed, and who is apt to be garrulous. The translator may be found to be quiet and unassuming, even if he, too, is able quickly to frame sentences and expressions for whatever he is asked to translate. He also is expected to understand and interpret what others may be thinking, without always being able to ask for an explanation, as the interpreter may do. By associating with the business executive, or conference members, on an almost equal footing, the interpreter willy-nilly acquires something of the same status. The translator is apt to be left out in the cold. Few see him, and, of course, still fewer know him as a person. His status is the undetermined one of the purely professional man.

This difference in status is often expressed unfortunately in terms of salary, the interpreter being paid considerably more than his colleague, for the reasons already explained. There appears to be no easy way to remedy this.

When we remember that a translator is often expected to attend meetings and take down the minutes, as a "précis writer," the difference in salary appears still more unfair.

Even odder is the fact that the translator may be called upon to interpret from time to time, or even regularly, without being paid as an interpreter. This has been my own lot, more than once. It is up to the translator and his professional associations, in such cases, to point out the anomalous position in which they find themselves.

Other requirements for those undertaking this career are that they should have done some foreign travel and have a fair degree of familiarity with the country concerned and its literature, plus a fairly wide culture. For these reasons, a university education is normally regarded as a good preparation for becoming a translator.

To tell the truth, a translator *can never know too much*. He is expected to be something in the nature of a walking encyclopedia; and not only to be able to use words, but to know what he is talking about, no matter how few others do!

Besides thumping with his shoe at the United Nations, Nikita S. Khrushchev was in the habit of producing Russian proverbs every now and then, as though to test his interpreters, who were sometimes hard put to it to find an English equivalent.

Thus we see why anyone who wishes to become a translator or interpreter should have a wide interest in all that goes on around him, as well as an interest in his own language. These are the most important qualifications. It goes without saying, of course, that next comes knowledge of at least one foreign language, and the more the better.

French is perhaps the most important for an English speaker from the international point of view, with Spanish a close second, and more important perhaps in commerce, at least as far as the American continent is concerned. These two, it should be noted, are official languages of the United Nations, as are Russian and Chinese.

Anyone with a gift for languages is well advised to learn Russian, as well as French and Spanish, because of its increasing importance as a language of science, and also because knowledge of this language is often a deciding factor when it comes to securing a job. Learning Russian is no more difficult than learning Latin, and much more fun.

Those who are gluttons for punishment might tackle Chinese, which will no doubt become more important in the future. A knowledge of Chinese can be gained at little cost by using the method recently developed by the Peking government,* though more profound knowledge will require some effort, since there are so many characters to be learned. By using cards, however, and constantly referring to them, in the bus, in a restaurant, when shaving, and at other odd moments, a surprising number of characters can be made familiar. For normal reading purposes a knowledge of 1,000 of these is essential, at least.

Other out-of-the-way languages that may prove useful to the interpreter in particular are Portuguese, a most pleasant variation of Spanish; German, important in the world of philosophy and science; or one of the African languages, say Swahili.

In discussing qualifications, therefore, it is well to remember that a university education is not always absolutely necessary. As we have seen, a translator is often called upon to do précis work; and there will be occasions when even a stenographer who knows shorthand will be asked to act as a précis writer, like a well-known free lance of my acquaintance, a woman with a most distinguished record, whose services are now sought after by half a dozen international organizations. The United Nations

---

* In the *Modern Chinese Reader,* Vols. I and II, Epoch Publishing House, Peking, 1958.

Educational, Scientific, and Cultural Organization (UNESCO) often must train précis writers in Paris, on the job, who are selected from among stenographers. Such persons, male or female, knowing one or two languages, will often find that their duties also include some translating. Like another woman of my acquaintance, they may thus become "translator/précis writers," in the U.N. classification, with or without a university education. Ambitious secretaries would do well to bear this possibility in mind! Although one is expected to be able to do both, in practice one does what one is best at, and there is little difference, really, between "précis work" and stenography, although précis writers probably will not agree!

Equally, an interpreter who knows one or two out-of-the-way languages, such as Russian, Chinese, or Hungarian, really well, will have little difficulty in finding a job. U.N. organizations everywhere will give such people a language test at once, and be only too glad to do so, so great is the need for their services.

One last point remains to be mentioned in this connection, and that is technical work. Here the question has been raised by employers as to who makes the better translator or interpreter: the trained linguist, usually an arts graduate, or the technical specialist, who knows one or two languages. There is no straight answer to this. Much depends upon circumstances. It may be stated, however, that in U.N. agencies and larger commercial concerns preference is generally given to the graduate in arts who is a trained linguist. The arts man is usually considered to have a wider culture and to be more experienced in purely linguistic techniques, semantics, lexicography, and so on.

It was found that in a field other than his own, the technical expert was often just as much at sea as the arts specialist, without having the latter's linguistic "know-how."

Technical experience, however gained, is of course invaluable for the technical translator. One of the finest translators of my acquaintance is an Englishman living in Geneva, who was an arts graduate but who worked as a student at the docks and in many branches of industry, thus gaining an insight into *processes* as well as special vocabulary. When he translated into English from French or German, he knew the subject at first hand in many cases and had no hesitation at times in writing a report, or abstract, instead of sticking to a purely verbatim translation.

To sum up then, a university education is the best existing form of preparation for the career of translator or interpreter, and preferably one leading to a professional degree in translation, as offered by a number of universities. In addition, as much technical knowledge as possible of actual industrial and scientific processes, tools, techniques, and vocabulary should be gained.

This is not to say that there is no other way of achieving one's goal. Women in particular, as we have seen, may progress from stenography through précis writing to translation work, but the wider one's knowledge the more qualified one is. *A translator can never know enough about anything* and should therefore be keenly interested in everything.

If he (or she) is ambitious, he should learn as many languages as possible—and a minimum of three; or else study profoundly one of the rare languages, such as Russian or Chinese.

The translator will tend to concentrate more on the written language, and will prefer to work alone. The interpreter will concentrate more on the spoken language, being fond of company and more "extrovert," though such terms have no absolute meaning.

Both will take a pride in their own language, since in practice they may use it more than the foreign one, as the "target" language into which they translate.

They will be interested, therefore, in language as such, and in communication as the most important problem of modern times—a subject leading to related fields, which will be dealt with in another chapter.

They will be interested in other people and how they live, and therefore fond of travel. They may even wish to live abroad for a while to perfect their knowledge of a country and its inhabitants. In so doing, they will also be ambassadors of their own country, which will be judged in the end not by its history, but by how its representatives behave.

Nor should it be forgotten, finally, that there is another side to the learning of foreign languages. English, to a foreign speaker, is the foreign language. The translator or interpreter finds to his surprise that the "foreign" language he knows best is his own! He becomes aware of a delightful choice facing him. He can either work at home, using his knowledge of the foreign language to earn his living, or he can go and work abroad, in any capacity, using his knowledge of English as a stepping-stone. This choice is not often realized by beginners. If he is true to his calling, he will not mind overmuch which he does, since in both cases he is serving the cause of human understanding.

Here we come to the most necessary requirement of all, and one that applies throughout life in many spheres: "You must like what you are doing."

When starting out on a career, remember, you are proposing to spend your life doing it. Whether you do so or not is beside the point. You may in fact find something related that you like better. But whatever you have chosen, you must like it so much that it hardly seems like work.

You are going to be doing it for a long while! Unless you are passionately fond of languages and travel, therefore, you would do much better to think of something else: some form of work in which you can use them as a sideline and an additional qualification.

If on the other hand, you are an enthusiast, read on!

CHAPTER II

*The Job—What It Is All About—
How to Do It*

Having acquired an idea of the qualities and attitudes needed in a translator or interpreter, we may well ask what exactly *is* translation? What, in fact, does a translator do?

The answer is not as easy as it seems. There are those, and eminent scholars among them, who maintain that it is impossible to translate from one language to another. They explain to us in detail that each language is a carefully structured system, like a code, and that it is encrusted with the tradition, customs, history, and psychology of those who speak it. Peoples may think entirely differently. They may build their sentences quite other than we do, with no subject, or with one word standing for a sentence, like the so-called agglutinative languages, of which Turkish is one.

To some extent this is true. Translation *is* impossible. Yet it is done every day. How, we may ask? How can it be done if it is impossible?

It may be said, here and now, that the very people who maintain it is impossible—linguistic scholars—are often also those most actively engaged in research to make it easy, and a mere matter of mechanics. So it cannot be all that impossible! They do not believe that translation is an art. It can be reduced, they say, to scientific principles. Well and good. So far, however, research into translation lags far behind other linguistic research, and the translator must carry on as best he can, *in practical work,* providing the grist for *their* mill.

It is true that language is a kind of code, and that a language does carry with it a whole way of thinking and feeling, a whole history and way of living—what we call the "American," or any other, way of life. Is that so terrible? Is it not a pleasure to acquire that way of life, by spending some time in the actual country?

There was a time when we were not so worried about such "codes," and when we referred to the "culture" of a country. The fact is that a language is the expression of a country's culture; and if we learn it, we thereby acquire a knowledge, however slight, of its culture. Perhaps the linguistic experts who on the one hand say that translation is not possible, and on the other try to invent forms of machine translation, have been misled into thinking that culture and language can be divorced. Linguistic experts are not necessarily noted for their knowledge of a country's *culture*. They are too apt to regard the "language" as the culture in microcosm, forgetting that the art, music, and literature of a country are as much part of the "language," or civilization, of that country, as the spoken language itself. Knowledge of a country's culture is thus indispensable to the would-be translator. He must be a sponge constantly soaking up facts, words, gestures, signs, and an entire climate.

All right, but what about translation? This may be of several kinds, literary, administrative, or technical.

Of these, literary translation is by far the most difficult and should not be undertaken by anyone unless he or she knows the source language thoroughly and has also a complete mastery of the target language. All too often translations are produced that greatly diminish the prestige of literary translation as against the others. I have seen a translation of a modern German novel by a distinguished English writer, in concert with a German, highly praised *as a translation,* while at the same time the novel was condemned as literature! Could obscurantism go further? In fact, of course, the translation is quite poor at times and does not at all reflect the qualities of the magnificent German original. But because the English "translator" is reasonably well known in England, it has been assumed that his work is above reproach. This is the kind of thing that erects barriers between countries and leads to statements such as the one we have seen, that translation is impossible.

There are, naturally, countless brilliant literary translations. Constance Garnett's translations of the Russian classics are models of their kind. German translations of Shakespeare, and also the late Boris Pasternak's translations of Shakespeare into Russian, are examples to be imitated. No doubt literary translation will go on to new heights and flourish as never before. It must do so indeed, if universal understanding is to be achieved. For those who would like to undertake this work, therefore, a few hints may be in order.

Generally, such translation has to be suggested to a publisher. One may come across a book, in French, Italian, or German, which has never been translated, and which is so good that it ought to be made available to the English-speaking world. The first thing to do in such a case is to write to the publisher, and to the author of the original, asking permission to publish an English translation and suggesting that the foreign firm may be willing to produce the book on its own. This is becoming increasingly the case. If the answer is that there is no objection to a translation, but that the translator must find an English-language publisher, the next step is to translate a chapter and send it, with an outline of the book concerned, to publishers in English who undertake this type of work. Now the question of payment arises. In the past, translators, especially when engaged by a publishing house direct, have usually been poorly paid, receiving a fixed sum for doing the entire book. This is not to be recommended, especially in the case of a high-quality English translation, which, if well done, is nothing less than a re-creation of the original work in English. For this, the translator, in my opinion, is entitled to as much as 10 percent of the royalties on the English edition. Actually, he will be lucky to earn 7½ percent—and normally will be offered 5 percent. Nevertheless, a percentage of royalties should be the goal, since, if the book sells over the years, as it ought to do if it is any good, the translator will also be receiving payment over the years for his initiative and his creative contribution.

How does he go about the actual work of translation? This is entering into discussion of the actual technique of translation, which is reserved for another chapter, but we can at least say that he must translate the *theme,* the *style,* and the *sense,* sticking to the original as closely as possible, but not producing a word-for-word translation, which is not a translation at all, and may even prove to be nonsense.

A famous example of this is the well-known word-for-word schoolboy translation of the French phrase, *"Voilà l'anglais avec son sang-froid habituel."*—"There is the Englishman with his usual bloody cold."

This leads us to one of the main principles of translation, which is to translate the whole and not the parts. Only when we have read through the text are we justified in splitting up sections for translation into sentences, or phrases, as the case may be.

No one knows, we are told, exactly what goes on in a translator's head when he translates from one language to another. This is flattering, but, of course, the translator himself might be asked once in awhile. No one knows in which part of the brain the information is stored, they say. Such questions do not worry the professional. *He,* at least, knows that he does not *think* his way from one language to another. He *feels* his way from one to another. He almost assumes a different personality when speaking the other language; and yet this is not true either. All that has happened is that he has developed and enriched his own. Here we put our finger on the secret of translation: it is to produce a "communication." In today's world of what are hopefully called "mass communications," translation—possibly the most important field of human communications, since there are over two thousand languages—is only beginning to be appreciated. Anything that can help communication, then, is translation, or interpretation. Gesture is part of language—called *kinesics.* Facial expression is part of language. Watch two people who do not speak each other's language trying to read each other's faces! Watch the antics of the clown in a circus! These gestures and expressions are now the subject of scientific study as a branch of linguistics. Interpreters and translators have been using them for centuries and have always maintained that you need to be "something of an actor" to speak another language. I would much rather say you need to have a broad, outgoing personality, with imagination and sympathy, to understand and share the experience of another human being, whatever his language. Surely, then, it is no miracle, but only a part of being human, to imitate, or to be able to converse or write in another language.

To ignore the human element is to ignore the dynamic and developing component in language itself, which is a living force, growing at fantastic speed. This is why dictionaries have been called "depositories of dead words." Human speech abandons some words and invents new ones daily. This is also why the future for machine translation is not too bright. The cost of following the fantastic changes in human speech, terminology, and grammar may prove much too costly. I am no expert, but to me, existing research is tragically wrong, blind, and even stupid. Years ago, had it developed along the lines of phonology, and on the lines of the telephone, it might by now have accomplished something, perhaps—but in the world of interpretation, not translation.

It is amusing to discover the difference between two speakers who do not know each other's language at all, and the conversation of two speakers in the same position who are *technicians*. In the latter case, technique serves as a language, because it is itself a form of communication. The first couple stare at each other, trying to read each other's features; they gesticulate, gesture, and are apt to shout; or to utter the words very clearly and slowly, which is useless. They turn to the interpreter as to a god, and yet go on watching the *face* of the other. The second couple are perfectly happy. They are in love with their trade. They do not even want an interpreter and angrily wave him away, maintaining that he will be no good because he does not understand the job. Actually, they have a point. Their own language, the trade, is better. They know it. Also, of course, they are having fun. The original "code"—words—has been abandoned with great glee. A point to remember. Another point to remember is that when an interpreter has brought such people together his job is done. He is a medium, nothing more.

Even when he interprets between two ordinary people, he must keep himself out. If he does not, he creates chaos. I saw an almost unbelievable instance of this at the end of the war. A private soldier who had a knowledge of several languages, including Russian, was selected to act as an interpreter at high-level meetings because of his knowledge of the Russian language. Instead of seizing the opportunity to "bring people together," he actually separated them! Whenever the U.S., British, and Soviet generals were together, this charming man would chat amicably with the Russian about everything from war aims to the state of the black market, only to be interrupted by one of the irate English-speaking generals.

"What does he say?" the general would ask, purple, only to be waved away with the airy reply, "Nothing."

This is a common tendency on the part of interpreters, to "hog" the scene. Needless to say, it has no future. Our man did not last long and was returned to his unit.

Translators face no such temptations. Their prosaic existence is rarely interrupted by anything glamorous, although it can happen that the world waits upon his translation of a text, whether the Coptic of a new archeological discovery, or the Vietnamese of a new threat to world peace.

Yes, one reason for the slowness of international negotiations is the fact that we do not have enough trained experts in translation!

The same principle applies to technical as to literary translations. "The first principle of good technical translating is to translate ideas and not words. When a competent translator sees the word 'Punktschweissmaschine,' it should serve to evoke before his mind's eye an image of something which he will then proceed to describe in English as a "spot-welding machine," but he should not merely equate these terms in the two languages without visualizing what they represent."*

All translation in fact requires a knowledge

a) of vocabulary,
b) of sentence structure (including cases, prepositions, verbs, conjunctions, and relative pronouns.)

Here is some advice for beginners, or those who must translate very difficult texts, or texts in a language that is not very well known:

---

* *Scientific and Technical Translating:* UNESCO, Paris, 1957: p. 31.

1. Trace the beginning and end of the sentence.
2. Split up the sentence into sections that can be analyzed separately. Watch here for commas, colons, semicolons, and such words as "that" or "which," etc., these being called "separators."
3. Watch out for the endings of verbs and the different tenses.
4. Group isolated words into syntagma, or systematic collection, using for this purpose any declensions, and noun, adjectival, or adverbial complements.
5. Watch out for the different cases in languages with declensions.

What this amounts to is simply, in the case of a long sentence, to split it up where commas or relative pronouns occur, and to translate the resulting phrases, remembering that it is the meaning of the whole that must be conveyed, rather than the meaning of the parts.

Caution and common sense are vital qualities in translation. One should beware of the obvious. One young man doing a U.N. test in Spanish, translated the word "bomba," not once, but several times, as "bomb," instead of simply "pump," making no effort to check. That failed him. Sensitivity to language itself would have saved him.

Whatever translation may be in theory, and however it may come to be regarded in practice, a definite technique, or working method, of translation has long been in existence.

Most translators first of all read the original right through, in order to get the feel of the context. In so doing, they underline any unknown or doubtful words. Dictionaries, cards, or specialists are then consulted for the unknown words. Next, they proceed to draft a first English version, usually straight onto the typewriter; or dictate it to a typist, or into a Dictaphone. This original draft is then gone over with great care, every *word* being examined and checked, especially those that are unknown or unfamiliar. The latter may need to be double-checked, against encyclopedias, manuals, or other colleagues. Due correction having been made, the final draft is then committed to paper, or dictated as previously. Any blanks that were left, for mathematical or other formulae, are now inserted by hand, in the final copy. THE FINAL COPY IS THEN GONE THROUGH AGAIN FOR ERRORS. It is surprising how many are to be found, even at this stage! Then the whole translation is read through once again for style and fluency, before being passed to the reviser, or otherwise checked out as approved.

The professional is well aware that there is often no similarity in linguistic contexts, for systems of ideas in one language may have no existence in another, and associations can be very different. A passage translated should nevertheless, ideally, read as if written in the language into which it has been translated.

We have mentioned consultation with colleagues in the case of difficulty, or consultation of lexicons, encyclopedias, or technical manuals and other material, for the purpose of checking and following specialized terminology.

This brings us to the question of dictionaries and documentation in general.

The professional translator will have at his disposal one or two carefully selected dictionaries: the English-French/French-English Harrap perhaps; Cassell's German, supplemented possibly by both of the *Duden* books, with illustrations; a Russian-English "Smirnitski"; as well as the dictionaries published by the U.S.S.R. Academy of Sciences. In Italian and Spanish almost any modern dictionary of reasonable dimensions is as good as another, but there is a dearth here. Ragazzini's Italian Dictionary is useful; so is Cassell's Italian and their Spanish Dictionary.

Those mentioned are standard works.* For technical purposes, the French-English/English-French Ketteridge Dictionary, published by Routledge, is extremely useful; and the C. G. King French-English "Electronics Dictionary," published by Dunod, Paris, is invaluable. Useful also are the Paterson French-English Chemical Dictionary, from Wiley and Sons; the Lépine French-English/English-French Medical and Biological Dictionary, and the general Chamber's Engineering Dictionary. In German, the German-English Technical Dictionary by de Vries, is useful, as is the Medical Dictionary by Schoenwald, published by Lewis, London.

---

* This list is not intended to be complete. A really exhaustive list would require a volume to itself. The dictionaries mentioned are, however, those most commonly used in practice and the most reliable. A fuller list is given in Appendix B.

In Russian, the peerless Callaham Russian-English Chemical and Polytechnical Dictionary is outstanding for work in almost any technology with engineering implications, including nuclear; and the English-Russian/Russian-English Electronics Dictionary, published by McGraw-Hill for the Department of the Army, Washington, D.C., is excellent in its field. Useful, too, is the Elsevier Nuclear Physics and Atomic Energy Dictionary in English, French, German, and Russian, although the U.N. Glossary of Nuclear Terms is far superior. A series of telecommunications dictionaries put out by Elsevier is not in practice helpful for anything remotely difficult. The Manual of Conference Terminology published by the same firm in Holland, on the other hand, is a good elementary guide for interpreters, including, as it does, most of the phraseology in the relevant languages.

Other indispensable scientific guides are Etherington's Nuclear Engineering Handbook, from McGraw-Hill; the Mining-Geological Dictionary by Novitzky, published in Buenos Aires; and the Voskobojnik, a first-class Russian-English Nuclear Dictionary published in Moscow, by Fifmatgiz, in 1961.

The dictionary of the International Electrotechnical Commission is standard, as is the Journal of the I.T.U., the International Telecommunications Journal.

This brings us to the second point, which is that it is impossible to rely on even the best of dictionaries, and supplementary aids must be discovered.

Inevitably the translator forms his own card index of expressions in the various disciplines he is working in. This is kept up-to-date, consulted, and altered regularly. Indeed, if a system of interchange of such card indexes could be arranged, all translators would benefit considerably, and the nucleus of a Terminology Library could be created that would be really useful and reflect current practice and research throughout the world.

Once the most relevant dictionaries and works of reference have been obtained and the card index has been set up, work can begin. Here *communication* involves also *information,* since, whether one is an expert or not, one must keep up-to-date.

This is not always easy. There are, it is true, the technical magazines, but they are limited and do not always provide the necessary phraseology in the foreign language. Useful therefore are the international publications available in several languages from international organizations. The I.T.U. *Journal,* already mentioned, published in English, French, Spanish, and Russian, is valuable. So also are the Information Sheets produced in English, French, and German by the Center for Industrial Safety (the International Occupational Safety and Health Information Service of the I.L.O.) in Geneva. These latter, I may say, are particularly valuable as providing the very difficult terminology involved in the various processes and sectors of industrial engineering and manufacture. The Food and Agriculture Organization (F.A.O.) in Rome regularly issues "World Fisheries Abstracts" in various languages.

Lists of similar publications in the various languages may be obtained directly from the United Nations, New York; in Canada, from the Queen's Printer, Ottawa; or from the International Civil Aviation Organization, Montreal; or from the World Health Organization, Geneva, Switzerland.

The general translator will also find it useful to keep up with current language and social developments as revealed in *Le Monde* and *Paris Match* (Paris); *Der Spiegel* (Germany); one of the Spanish journals, *España,* perhaps; and English and Russian editions of the *Soviet Union,* for comparison of the language used.

When some sort of specialization intervenes, as it is almost bound to do in the course of time, then the abstracts of the proceedings of chemical, biological, or other scientific societies throughout the world will provide a fund of valuable information and reference.

Nevertheless, it is impossible for one person to keep abreast of everything. For this reason, the possibility of consulting a panel of experts of one's acquaintance, in various disciplines, becomes of urgent importance. Whether or not they are acquainted with several languages, they can be a constant help, and a form of insurance also, when in doubt.

The basic problems are the same in the case of private translating bureaus, international organizations, and translation schools; that is, to create the proper organization first, so as to have available at all times a developing picture of what is going on in technical processes and research, together with a growing vocabulary to accompany it.

In practice, translation work is graded in order of difficulty, and thus itself also grades translators. Work is checked carefully by the actual translators, not once, but many times. All the available dictionaries, documentation, files, literature, indexes, and consultants, are utilized before a translation is finally passed to the reviser. The latter, normally someone who has spent many years in his work as a translator, may be a technician, but more likely is not, his knowledge having been acquired by experience and by technical reading, so that in fact he may be indistinguishable from the technician as far as his knowledge of the subject is concerned.

His is the final responsibility for the draft which in the end is issued, and it may differ very considerably indeed from the original translated version; almost as much, in fact, as any version produced by mechanical methods! Except that the machine cannot in the nature of things consult advisers by telephone, or thumb through a week's issue of a technical journal to find a totally new expression, of which there are thousands.

All the machine can do at present is produce a version that must be carefully checked for serious errors by a translator before going any further. It thus upgrades translators and makes them into revisers, which may be all to the good, though for many years to come the ordinary work of the translator will not be affected at all, if indeed it ever is.

The fact that work varies in difficulty is also the reason why output varies with the type of text to be translated and the working conditions provided. Working on a text of average difficulty, with expert secretarial assistance, the translator may be able to produce 2,000 words per day. If the text is highly technical, or if the translator must supervise the typing, or check stencils himself, his output may not exceed 1,000 words. These are only approximate figures. Many organizations claim to expect 3,000 to 4,000 words per day! Translators should and do resist any attempt to standardize "production" in such an unintelligent way, yet "costing" demands that for some reason the translator's work be counted, graded, sifted, and calculated, as though he were a journalist being paid a penny a line. This may be a hangover from the publishing or newspaper worlds. Interpreters are not so treated. Be that as it may, estimates of production are not hard and fast, although they generally do settle, for international organizations, at around 7 to 10 pages of fairly normal text per day.

On the other hand, I have spent one week on a paragraph! Admittedly, it was of considerable technical difficulty.

Although translators are not necessarily expected to type their own translations, many of them do. It is in the interests of employers to provide efficient secretaries, and typewriters with suitable keyboards! Many people apparently do not realize that there are different keyboards for different languages. Provision of an efficient secretary can raise a translator's output to as much as 6,000 words per day! This, however, is by no means to be regarded as a desirable average, as it means working at top speed, often without a break of any kind.

As regards references, all conference documents, background information, and reference material should be made available to the translator, and normally are, in efficient organizations. It is important that translators should be made to feel that they are in the picture as much as interpreters, and not victims of "out-of-sight, out-of-mind" judgments. Much, if not all, may depend on their work when it comes to the actual text of such things as treaties, commercial agreements, business contracts, markets, specifications, and so on. If this were generally realized by those concerned with "progress" in various fields, there is no doubt whatsoever that the status of the translator would be much higher than it is at present.

Such documentary information is indispensable to a translator in his work, although many employers appear to think he possesses a private crystal ball. Is it possible that many hard-headed businessmen still believe in magic? I doubt it. Let them therefore cheerfully make available to the translator every facility he demands, within reason. It will pay off in the end, and handsomely.

It would also help translators considerably if conference organizers could send a full list of conference documents well in advance of meetings, so that they may familiarize themselves with the subject matter.

Finally, since noise and interruptions reduce output, translators do need offices, preferably to themselves, where they can work undisturbed. Their work resembles that of watchmakers in its need for accuracy!

Précis writers require the same working conditions as translators. A team of three members is needed to cover a normal three-hour meeting, and attendance at the meeting and the subsequent drafting of the record represent at least a full day's work for each of the précis writers concerned. If one meeting per day is held, then one précis-writing team is required; if two meetings, two teams; and so on.

It is a sad commentary on the neglect of the profession that it should be necessary to write such things at all, yet such is the case, especially in many otherwise respectable companies.

All this would seem to indicate that more time and attention should be spent in universities in turning out professional translators who will be aware and proud of their status, as the *only links* between what C. P. Snow has perhaps mistakenly called the "two cultures," *i.e.,* the scientific and the literary.

The technical translator must be conversant with the basic terminology and discipline of the science he works in, and just as some "culture" may rub off on the science student who takes an English course, so some scientific "culture" may rub off on the translator who has been an arts student. He will become aware of the general utility, and the social as well as other implications of scientific work, which the pure science student has generally little time to contemplate.

Thus the translator, technical or not, is, as his title implies, a bridge, and a vital one today within our social system, not only between the "two cultures," but also between many opposing groups, inside and outside national boundaries. Upon his work depends, to a large extent, world understanding and therefore, also, world peace, as the Peace Corps in the United States is well aware.

CHAPTER III

*The Nature of Language—Speaking
and Writing—Some Qualitative Aspects
of Translation and Interpretation*

It is generally accepted today that language is not simply a form of speech that happens to be used in everyday life. The concept of language now embraces every form of communication, spoken or written; alphabetical or symbolical; artistic or mathematical. Many prominent authorities, in fact, consider that mathematical symbols may in the end come to dominate other forms of communication, as they now tend to do in the higher branches of economics, linguistics, and physics where an "equation" may give us the formula for solar activity, or a complete representation of English syntax.

To me, I confess, there is something rather specious about this. Even mathematical symbolism is simply one form of language among many. Let us examine some of the others.

It is well known that our alphabet, as a system of writing, developed out of ancient forms similar to the rune, hieroglyphics, Chinese, and other forms of pictorial writing. There is no time here to go into the fascinating growth of the Roman alphabet, or even the Cyrillic. All that is intended is to stress that the idea of phonetic letters grew out of symbols. Many such symbols remain alive today and enrich our language. Think of all the printer's symbols, traffic symbols, semaphore, Morse, Braille, and heraldry—each with its own symbolic language, conveying not merely a picture, but meaning, or image. In some forms of Aztec and Mayan, indeed, it is difficult to decide if we are dealing with a letter or with a pictorial symbol, so complicated is the image. It resembles, indeed, much of modern art. This form of communication by sign or symbol has even given rise to a new science called semiotics. Once thought of as primitive, such symbols have once again come to be recognized as a form of *shorthand* for conveying messages. The image is quicker than the sentence. It is more concrete and specific than the mathematical equation. It is just as likely, therefore, that the image, and not the mathematical symbol, will dominate our epoch in the end. The mathematical symbol is abstract. It may convey a great deal, but it is a repository of meaning, like the dictionary; not a "universal message," like the image.

Primitive cave drawings in France and primitive forms of message or symbol in Siberian folklore make us feel that even art perhaps, had its origin in such symbols. There is little point therefore in saying, as do some scholars, that art was "originally abstract," because originally it was not art but *language*: an *image,* with a specific reference. The living line conveying the message was later isolated in "art," and came to have a career of its own, but it was never necessarily "abstract." On the contrary, it was probably always an expression of the *feeling* of the person who traced it. This, indeed, is its only link with art, and vitiates much of the so-called art of today, in which there is no longer any organic link between line and artist; where nothing is felt, no individual "handwriting," as we have come to say, exists; and therefore nothing is communicated. Yet art is basically also a form of communication. Today it is even turning back to the original hieroglyph from which it descended, as we can see from the work of such artists as Paul Klee, or Joan Miró. The image has become discredited perhaps, in art, yet the original hieroglyph remains, in all its purity.

Gesture, too, is part of language, and the study of gesture has produced yet another science still in its infancy. Kinesics is concerned with the link between word and gesture, and with the significance of gesture in a culture: why it should be rude in one culture to belch, and polite in another, as among the Eskimos; why it should be rude in one country to put out one's tongue, and polite in another; why some cultures use more gestures than others, and so on. Again, we have no time to go into this fascinating side of language, but it may be useful to interpreters to be aware that what can be expressed by a shrug is also language.

Human speech, too, has an infinite number of sounds, all of

them part of language, from the guttural "r" of French, to the Zulu click; even whistling has become a language on its own in the Canary Islands. Such sounds can be faithfully reproduced through the science of phonology, and it is the function of language laboratories to enable students to reproduce them without self-consciousness. Study of phonology, therefore, and even of voice production can be of great assistance to interpreters, who rely on their voices. Any self-consciousness is merely failure to understand that forms of communication are in fact language. It is perhaps also due to a belief that there is some magic "standard" in one's own language or in a foreign language, not to reach which is failure. This is false. One may be near or far from native speech, but communication is the vital thing. Every aid toward it is language.

Phonology thus studies the nature of sounds and enables us to reproduce them with the aid of the *written* symbols of phonetics.

Then, of course, there are the specialized "languages" of science. Our doctor may tell us what is wrong with us, but he too often does not communicate and must "translate" into English. This is not because we are stupid or uneducated, but because he has a language of his own, medical language. The botanist can name any flower we wish, but it says nothing to us unless he "translates" it into some popular name of which we have heard. Again this is because he has his own language of classification, largely artificial or synthetic, which he has had to develop for his own purposes in order to describe an infinite variety of which we have no conception.

There are also mathematical languages, biological, engineering, mechanical, and geological languages *within* our own language, whatever that may be. Often we refer to them as jargon, but they become jargon only when they invade or usurp the world of common speech. So many forms of language exist, in fact, that sometimes we hear talk of a "crisis of language," which may or may not be just another alarm. If we remember, however, that our speech is only one form of language, we shall see that there is, in fact, little cause for alarm. Whatever the crisis—and it sometimes takes the form of a "crisis," or even "breakdown," in communication between young and old, black and white, East and West, art and science—it need not be taken too seriously. Strictly speaking, the word "communication" is being used here in a metaphysical sense. Breakdown thus expresses the idea of "having nothing in common," with which we have nothing to do, since language is common to us all. Belief, or faith, or a common goal, is not language, although it may have a language. As far as pure communication is concerned, communication embraces all forms of language, as we have seen, and cannot now be interrupted or suspended. The process of human integration, reinforced by speech, the written word, music, the arts, and technology, is irreversible; and every form of "metaphysic," from "young" and "old," "black" and "white," "left" and "right," or "East" and "West" to philosophical and religious prejudice, will be obliged to yield to it. One of the translator's proudest tasks, indeed, is to help in this integration, and to know that he does so as a *person,* not as a link in a mechanical chain or process. He stands at the crossroads between machine domination of environment, or a synthetic world, including man; and a human world, with human control of the machine; between war, as we have said, and peace; for these alternatives are almost synonymous.

Language, both human speech and written language, soon developed its own cult known as "letters"; and the "man of letters" became a "littérateur," just as "letters" became "literature." All well and good. The poem, the novel, the short story flourished in this world, the world of the printed word. If we are to believe Marshall McLuhan, however, all is no longer well with that world. Electronics is with us, and TV. We live in an electric world that has become the extension of the human nervous system. But is this not what we stated at the beginning of this chapter? That "art" is the extension of the line? And of the image symbol? An extension in fact of the "nervous" system? Any extension of the nervous system, indeed, will produce art, insofar as it is integrated. "Nervous system," incidentally, is not too good an expression; "living organism" might be better. So our electric environment produces TV and the cinema, both the subject of study by the new science of semiotics, the language of signs and symbols. *"Plus ça change, plus c'est la même chose,"* we might say. Language is still with us, whether spoken or written; and the electric environment may be expected to produce a new and better form of writing, or art, or literature, but only if it is as sensitive as eye, hand, and brain.

These various specialized languages may be summed up in the one word, *terminology*. Use the right word—and open sesame!—the magic door opens of itself.

Terminology is becoming more and more specialized, more and more "technical," and this is still another opportunity for the translator. He may never master a specialization, yet through experience and practice he may come to master quite a number of various terminologies, particularly with the aid of good technical dictionaries. In the future, too, he will be able to use tools such as the Dicautom system of automatic dictionaries developed by the Bureau de Terminologie of the European Coal and Steel Community of the European Commission, in collaboration with the Centre de Linguistique Automatique of the University of Brussels, Belgium.

This latter system has perhaps the greatest future in the field, and we may confidently look forward to the establishment of national terminological bureaus, based on programmed computers, linked up to an international terminological institute run perhaps by the United Nations, from which it will be possible in a matter of minutes to send the right technical expression to any country in the world. Is this not already a new form of the written word?

In addition to these artificial or technical languages, naturally, are the languages of human speech, of which there are approximately 3,000 throughout the world. These are largely grouped already into families, such as the Afro-Asiatic, the Altaic (Turkic, Mongolian, etc.), Caucasian, Indo-European, Niger-Congo, Sino-Tibetan, Aztec-Tanoan, and many others. No one can know them all. And in any case, what does "knowing" a language mean?

The Peace Corps in the United States has classified proficiency as follows:

S-1: Able to satisfy routine travel needs;
S-2: Able to meet routine social demands and limited work requirements;

S-3: Able to speak the language with sufficient structural accuracy and vocabulary; and

S-4: Able to use the language fluently and accurately on all levels normally relevant to professional needs.

This last is the standard normally to be aimed at. It does not equal native or bilingual proficiency, but is acceptable in translation work.

The problem then becomes one of selection. Which languages should be learned? In 1961, Peace Corps volunteers learned 15 different languages among them. By the end of 1968, however, the Peace Corps will have trained over 50,000 Americans in 150 languages, as part of their preparation for service in 65 countries. This is a feat worthy of acclaim and shows the vast field open to the translator or interpreter interested in doing something "different" and, indeed, pioneer work. These languages are too numerous to list here, but they include such little-known tongues as Pashto (Afghanistan), Douala (Cameroon), Yoruba (Dahomey), Amharic (Ethiopia), Mam (Guatemala), Telegu (India), Tagalog (Philippines), Wolof (Senegal), and Bobo (Upper Volta), as well as "normal" Spanish (Bolivia, British Honduras, Chile, Colombia, Costa Rica, Dominican Republic, Ecuador, El Salvador, Guatemala, Guyana, Morocco, Panama, Paraguay, Peru, Uruguay, Venezuela).

The widespread currency of Spanish, even where it is not the native language, reveals some need for selection. So does the United Nations, the "official" languages of which are English, French, Spanish, Russian, and Chinese. The student would therefore be well advised to make sure he is familiar at least with the first three of these, as the most commonly spoken. The addition of Russian would be extremely valuable, and/or Chinese, if possible. In international agencies it will be found that most translators can speak or read the first four, to a greater or lesser extent, either Spanish or Russian being less well known, perhaps, than the first two.

English, incidentally, has many forms, including what is known as "pidgin," * and also "bèche-la-mar." An acquaintance

---

* Originally meaning "business."

of mine in New Caledonia, selected for his excellent knowledge of French, discovered to his surprise and horror that he was expected to translate from "pidgin" English into French! Worse still, he also interpreted! This in spite of the difference we have noted, that the translator works from a written text into his mother tongue as a rule.

Having selected which languages he intends to work in, the student will need to become acquainted with what is involved. On the technical side, he should be aware that 50 percent of scientific literature is in languages that more than half of the world's scientists cannot read! He may therefore decide to specialize in technical work.

This decision may be reinforced by such facts as the following. It is probable that "practically all Russian scientists are able to read at least one foreign language with proficiency, the sequence being 'German, English, French' with a tendency to become 'English, German, French.'" *

This implies that "many more Russians than Germans can read Scientific German, that twice as many Russians as Frenchmen can read Scientific French, and that scientists able to read English total two-fifths as many in the U.S.S.R. as in the United States and the British Commonwealth put together." *

There are estimated to be some 1,000,000 scientists and technologists in the U.S.S.R., or five-sixths as many per thousand as in the United States. Of these, some 600,000 can read German; 500,000, English; and 400,000, French. The figure for U.S. and British scientists who can read foreign languages is much lower. In the United States, for instance, only about 90,000 can read German; 45,000, French; 905,000, English; and only 1,000 can read Russian! Some 30,000 can read Spanish, as compared with 50,000 in the Soviet Union. In view of the scientific advances in the U.S.S.R., these figures are hardly satisfactory for the West, and once more stress the need for translators in large numbers. The figures for the United Kingdom are better, but make little difference: there, 50,000 scientists can read German; 50,000, French; and 3,000, Russian.

It is no answer to say that most of the scientific literature in

---

* *Scientific and Technical Translating,* UNESCO, Paris,

the world appears in English. What matters is not quantity but quality.

In any case the quantity in Russian is impressive: of 1,000 scientific periodicals selected at random, the result was as follows for coverage:

Pure and Applied	English	Russian*	German	French	Spanish
Sciences in general	32	11	8	8	5
Mathematics, Astronomy, etc.	24	5	10	9	1
Geology and Mining	25	18	13	14	7
Medicine	78	13	28	22	16
Biology, Botany, Microbiology, Bacteriology, etc.	43	13	18	10	6

This is not a full table. Details may be obtained from the UNESCO volume *Scientific and Technical Translating*. These figures suffice, however, to show that the amount of scientific literature appearing in Russian is considerable; and the amount published in Spanish as regards medicine will not go unobserved.

Much of this literature is translated and available today from various translating agencies, including the Pergamon Institute in New York, and from government and other agencies. Some of these are listed in the Appendix. Such work is often done on a free-lance basis, although permanent staffers are also employed. For this purpose registers of specialist translators are maintained by the governments of the United States, Canada, and the United Kingdom, and work is farmed out to them at regular intervals. The international organizations, which must be in the vanguard, organizing conferences, symposia, and seminars of research workers throughout the world, have, of course, their own staffs and carry out their own vital translation and

---

* Including languages in Cyrillic script.

publishing work. It is perhaps high time that all this activity was properly centralized on a world basis.

In addition to these are countless private translating bureaus, some very bad, and many today exceedingly good. They, too, have their registered free-lance translators, who do work for them at regular intervals in the various languages required. It will be seen from this that even in the case of the normal translator some specialization is desirable.

Texts requiring translation vary both in content and in type of document. They may be divided into those that represent new knowledge in the field, and descriptions of its application in practice; reviews of existing knowledge and experience; educational material; and documents relating to engineering and industry. The first category includes papers in the proceedings of learned societies and technical institutions. The second comprises articles in scientific and technical, as well as general, journals; pamphlets, reports, and reference manuals. To the third belong syllabuses, certificates, and diplomas; textbooks and popular science publications; and finally, contracts and specifications; reports on tests and analyses; trade and commercial catalogues; publicity and directories; patent specifications; and national standards and international standardizing recommendations.

All of them include legal and literary material, as well as technical work.

To some extent we have already dealt with the actual technique of translating, and the facilities that should be placed at the translator's disposal. Terminology is a difficulty that is usually overcome by consulting the relevant documents. Card indexes should also be set up by all translators, in which every new term or expression is entered as it appears.

Collaboration is sometimes a necessity, and work is often divided between one or more translators. Care should be taken with the conversion of abbreviations, measurements, symbols, place names, and titles, for which adequate dictionaries are normally available. Some of these have been listed in the Appendix. Place names in general are left untranslated, the usual name, if well known, being shown in brackets, thus: Al Kahira (Cairo). As far as measurements and symbols are concerned, care should be taken to see that the correct symbol is given in the translation. Thus in French:

E_b, E_a, meaning *"coefficient d'elasticité du beton, de l'acier,"* should become in English E_c, E_s, standing for "the modulus of elasticity of concrete or of steel."

And in writing trigonometrical symbols the Germans use "tg" where in English we write "tan." Such tricky points are to be carefully watched for.

As we have seen, a good translator translates ideas, not words. He should be versed in and able to reason about the subject matter of the translation. If he is not, he may read up on the subject from documents or textbooks before starting work. He should be able to read the language he is translating well enough to distinguish the meaning even if it is badly expressed. This is an important point in a world where expression is by no means all it might be. *"Le mot juste"* is not always used! Finally the translator must also be able to embody the meaning in lucid, terse, and euphonious English prose.

Nor should the wording of the original carry forward into the English. Many words in French (for example, *actuel, assurer, brutal, demander, délai, éventuel, important, intéressant,* etc.) are similar in form to English words, but have a subtle difference in meaning. *"Actuel"* refers to the present, as any good translator knows. And *"demander"* is not "to demand," but only "to request." Even *"important"* is usually equal to "considerable." These are tricks of the trade. Similarly, the German word *"beide"* should not always be translated as "both," since often it merely means "the two." This will avoid such absurd sentences as "Both compounds are different." *"Sogenannte"* is not merely "so-called," but has something of the meaning of "alleged." Apart from these, the translator will tend in any case to search out expressions or words more English or American than he might otherwise use, in order to avoid giving the reader the feeling that the passage has been translated from French or German, or whatever the original language is. While so doing, however, he must not distort the original meaning by a hairsbreadth.

If no documentation is readily available, it may be possible, as has been said, to check on terminology by consulting encyclopedias, technical dictionaries, and abstracts of technical proceedings, or even bibliographies. If possible, however, a translator should be able to *visualize* the material, equipment, plant, or processes described. This is done best of all by visiting the site, but it may be assisted by photographs or illustrations. It is for this reason that pictorial dictionaries on the lines of the German *Duden* are useful, as are all photographs and specifications supplied.

All vocabulary invariably advances, and it is difficult to follow such evolution in detail unless some specialization is undertaken. On the other hand, this development itself militates against mechanical translation, and favors the human translator.

What has been said here about translating applies equally to interpreting, although differences exist between the two as regards technique.

There is less demand for interpreters from translation agencies, unless these happen also to arrange conferences. International business organizations, however, tend to be more interested in interpreters for their conferences, which they themselves arrange. They often have their own translators, and sometimes expect them to interpret also. For conferences, however, they do employ free-lance interpreters, and often translators as well, since additional ones are needed for the extra work.

As we have seen, a translator may set up his own private translation bureau. This the interpreter cannot do. He must work under contract, permanent or temporary, although, as we have also seen, he is much better paid.

Nevertheless, there is a tendency to expect the impossible from the interpreter also. It may come as a surprise to discover that at an important postwar conference between the Foreign Ministers of the United States, the U.S.S.R., the United Kingdom, and France, one interpreter was expected to function throughout for all four powers; yet he was paid by one government only! I can name his name, and the country that supplied him, and even his later modest reward. This sort of thing today would be indefensible, yet it still may occur in emergencies. I myself have attended meetings where I was expected to interpret into English from three foreign languages at the same time, and was criticized into the bargain! But one male interpreter for a top-level four-power conference! I venture to think that it is not now conceivable.

A woman of my acquaintance, who shall also be nameless, not only works regularly as a top-level technical interpreter—and thus must assimilate technical terminology regularly, at conferences and meetings that never seem to be dealing with the same subject—but is often called upon also to translate *from* and *into* Russian, and sometimes also into French and/or German. I have often wondered whether the best way to achieve peace would not be for all interpreters and translators throughout the world to go on strike until disarmament was carried out! Some of them have grounds for doing so, but I have never heard of any who did. I feel sure the public would not object, in any country!

In case it may be thought that an interpreter is simply somebody who can "play phonograph records in his head," let us examine what an interpreter is called upon to do. If he is performing simultaneous translation, then he must actually translate while the foreign speaker is talking. This is done by a system of interpreters' booths as operated in the United Nations, for example. The interpreter sits in a glass-enclosed booth and listens through earphones to the foreign speaker. At each minor pause, or when he considers suitable, he speaks into a relay-speaker, which relays his own voice to those in the audience or conference who are tuned in to "English." These delegates then hear the interpreter's voice, not that of the foreign speaker; and they hear the translation while the speech is actually in progress. The demands this makes on the interpreter as regards accuracy, presence of mind, quickness of wit, and vocabulary must be seen to be believed. Generally, he is able to cope because he knows the subject matter of the conference, the chit-chat, the arguments put forward and so on, and he has been fully briefed by his superior.

To some extent, however, the second type of interpretation is actually more nerve-wracking. I refer to "consecutive" translation, or translation when the speaker has concluded. Since this system wastes much time, it is not often employed at large conferences, but it is still quite common. In this case the interpreter has to wait until the speaker has completed his immediate statement. If

THE NATURE OF LANGUAGES 47

A meeting of the United Nations Fifth Committee.

UNITED NATIONS

the peroration is prolonged, as it can be, the interpreter must either store the material in his head, summarize it there, and then speak; or else take notes. It is inevitable that in the end he will find himself obliged to take notes, and they, moreover, must be swift, brief, and yet full! To do this he must employ either shorthand or a modified form of it. As in the case of précis writing, oddly enough, shorthand is not always considered an advantage here, because it means that the notes are too full! Details may be included that both speaker and interpreter know to be irrelevant, or tactless, or otherwise undesirable. These must be omitted. The précis writer in particular must take notes from which later to write up the minutes of the meeting, and minutes are not the same as a verbatim record, as we shall discover in the next chapter. When there are also interpolations, the situation is indeed difficult all around!

Interpreters are thus obliged to evolve their own system of note-taking, or to adopt a variation of one commonly employed in conferences, in which signs or letters stand for proposals, or countries, and so on. We are, in fact, back at the science of semiotics!

Some of these signs are as follows:

Mathematical:

$$\longleftarrow \text{ from, } \longrightarrow \text{ to,}$$

$$=, +-, \div \quad \times \quad : \quad > \quad < \quad ;$$

as short forms of

phrases, the latter meaning "greater than" and "less than."

Abbreviations:

R Russian US United States UK United Kingdom
F France

Thus we have, instead of:

"*The United States proposed to the U.S.S.R. that . . .*"

only: "US $\longrightarrow$ R";

THE NATURE OF LANGUAGES

and for: *"Control be established":*

"CONT. . . ."

"over the peaceful uses of atomic energy"

becomes:

"peace, atom."

Most interpreters or even précis writers evolve their own system, in practice, but details of the main lines of such "speed-writing" can be found in many guides, including those mentioned in the Appendix.

A sentence such as:

"The Soviet Delegate stated that his country's contribution was greater than that of the United States"

might thus be written:

"Ac   Sov. D. *their* cont.   >   US cont."

The only limitation on contractions, in fact, is the possibility of reading them back. What looks good at the time, when fresh in mind, may later be incomprehensible. So do not be too cryptic!

CHAPTER IV

The Main Field and the People in It— Précis Writing—The Communication Field

Translation as such is theoretically a part of the scientific study known as Applied Linguistics, and indeed a form of Comparative Linguistics. Although there is no need for a translator to know linguistics, some study of this subject cannot but be of use to him in his work, since it will make him more conscious of, and therefore more confident in, what he is actually doing.

Comparative linguistics, as the term implies, is concerned with comparing two or more languages from one or more points of view; and with the techniques that may be applied to such comparison. It therefore helps the translator in making him aware of the different approaches of such tongues as English and French, in the well-known example concerning crossing a river. Whereas English says: "He swam across the river," French says: *"Il traversa la rivière à la nage."*

English is concerned with the type of action. It leaves the purpose vague, and even the kind of river is not specified. In French we are told that he "crossed the river by swimming," and it is understood that the river was not a particularly wide one, such as might be indicated by the word *"fleuve."* Although the translator should be aware of such differences, comparative linguistics, and in particular comparative stylistics, will help him to become more wary of them.

It will also help him to realize that what he must translate is not the words, but the *meaning*. In linguistics, or the science of language, that branch which is concerned with meaning is called "semantics." This, too, is a subject to which the translator might give some attention. Not only will it assist him to discover meaning, but it will also make him more aware of the fact that meaning is found, not so much in individual words, as in how they are used in a particular *context*.

Questions of translation, indeed, are closely connected with semantic analysis and the contextual theory of meaning, as we saw when discussing the actual operation of translation step by step. In the words of the anthropologist Bronislaw Malinowski, indeed, translation implies "the unification of cultural context."

Just as we discovered that the work of translation makes us aware of foreign cultures, so now we are made to realize that, in fact, a foreign culture is actually the context of the language from which we are translating.

When we are dealing with the more familiar languages of Western Europe the difficulty of translation is not too great, because they have in common a unified cultural area, or context, at least to some extent. Working on languages whose speakers are culturally remote from Europe, however, such as Far Eastern languages, we realize the need for contextual explanations of meaning, and footnotes may be required to provide these.

It has been pointed out that single lexical equivalents are difficult when cultural unity is lacking. Religious communities may have their own type of language; and words such as *freedom, democracy,* or *equality* may mean different things on the two sides of the border between Communist and capitalist Europe. Hard work is sometimes required therefore to make clear precisely what a certain word may mean, if it has no exact equivalent in a different cultural context.

Study of semantics has produced in this connection the interesting theory of the *linguistic field,* or the *field theory of meaning.* This is concerned with showing that the lexical content of a language, or its total vocabulary, is not simply a conglomeration of independent items, as many people are apt to think, but that word-meaning is the contribution a word makes to the meaning of the sentence in which it appears. Words are not simply names of things, or "nomenclature," but are functions in a context.

In the old days language learning was pursued through the study of "grammar." Today, the emphasis has swung away from "grammar" toward fluency in speaking, laboratory drill, and the learning of phrases. "Grammar" then follows as an explanation of what has already been learned.

"Grammar" is also part of linguistics, and for the translator it is a vital part. Translation from Russian, in particular, depends to a large extent on how well one knows the endings of words, including verb and case endings, upon which meaning depends.

Bilingual speakers, those lucky people who grow up speaking two languages, learn such grammar, and "field meanings," early in life; but even in their case, study of phonetics, semantics, and comparative linguistics constitutes a useful background to the actual task of translating from one language to another, since again, it makes many unconscious processes more conscious, and allows intelligence to come into play.

Those who learn languages, instead of acquiring them early in life, are for this reason at no real disadvantage as compared with bilingual speakers, except possibly in the field of interpreting, where considerable fluency is required.

Even interpreters should have some acquaintance with linguistics, notably phonetics, phonology, and voice production.

These various studies will be dealt with again later in the section dealing with training. Here it is enough to point out that the main field with which we are concerned, translation and interpreting, forms part of what is called Applied Linguistics, as opposed to pure theory. It is an essentially practical field, concerned with meaning, the conveying of meaning, and communication in general.

The advantage possessed by native speakers over those who have learned a language in school is thus seen to be a contextual one. Modern training is reducing the gap through laboratory work and, above all, travel.

Translation, however, is a constant challenge, whether a language has been learned in childhood or at school.

One of the attractions of the career we are discussing is thus due to the fact that the people working in it come from various linguistic and ethnic backgrounds, and indeed from all over the world. Some of them may speak English, and another language—Italian, German, French, or even Russian—at home. It is true that Slavs make excellent linguists, but there is no truth in the oft-repeated statement that English speakers are poor linguists. Like the man who did not know whether he could play the piano, it is simply that they have rarely tried. When they do, they are as good as anyone else.

It is a cosmopolitan field, and the world of tomorrow in microcosm. In it we find world travelers; people with adventurous interests; expert technicians; writers; poets; and others interested enough in their fellow men to wish to work with them in the widest possible fashion.

First, there is what we may call the international group, made up of the many employees, some of them temporary, or seconded, of organizations such as the United Nations in New York; or the European office of the U.N. in Geneva, Switzerland; or UNESCO in Paris; the International Labor Organization (I.L.O.), the International Telecommunication Union (I.T.U.), the World Health Organization (W.H.O.), the World Meteorological Organization (W.M.O.), all in Geneva, Switzerland; as well as the International Atomic Energy Agency (I.A.E.A.), in Vienna, Austria; the International Civil Aviation Organization (I.C.A.O.), Montreal, Canada, and many others, such as the Inter-Governmental Committee for European Migration (I.C.E.M.), the U.N. Industrial Development Organization (U.N.I.D.O.), the U.N. Conference on Trade and Development (U.N.C.T.A.D.), and the Inter-Governmental Maritime Consultative Organization (I.M.C.O.), details and addresses of which may be found in the Yearbook of International Organizations, published annually and obtainable at most reference libraries.

All of these organizations employ a permanent staff of translators and interpreters, and also additional temporary staff, or "free lances," for their annual general conferences.

Even at home, increasing knowledge of language is required and therefore, to some extent, also translation work. The United States borders on Mexico, and the whole continent of South America must be its vital concern. A knowledge of Spanish and Portuguese (for Brazil) is therefore the first priority, one may say, for a translator in the United States, just as in Canada the priority must be French. The old "foreign correspondent" in commerce has not been superseded by any means. His work has expanded enormously. Over and beyond commercial correspondence and publicity material, both of which require slanting toward the native speaker, a great amount of literary translation remains to be done from Spanish and French. This involves, as we have seen, a knowledge of the history, culture, and traditions, not to say the psychology, of the nationality concerned. It is perhaps not an exaggeration to say that much of the apparent "unrest" in foreign countries has resulted from the blind impact of technology of foreign cultures, with no appreciation, understanding, or knowledge of the language concerned, or of how the way of life may be affected by new media. If this is to be corrected, translation into and from these languages must be furthered in every possible way.

Not only literary, but also educational materials require translation: foreign-language textbooks must be drafted, or translated, since many written abroad are superior to those written at home. One of the best books on Scientific Russian to come to my knowledge, for instance, was originally written in French and needed to be translated by myself before it could be used in English-speaking countries. I refer to the work by Y. Gentilhomme, published by Dunod, Paris.

The main field of translation work, then, is as wide as human culture itself. Our world is shrinking, owing to technological advance, and it has become a matter of survival that we should know and understand how our neighbors, and even distant cousins, think and feel.

In addition to translators, of course, international concerns increasingly employ secretarial staff, stenographers, personnel officers, information officers, editors, publications advisers, public-relations officers, accountants, clerks, and others too numerous to name, all of whom must have a knowledge of at least one language other than their own, which they use in some approximation to translation work. There are library services; educational services; printing and publishing services; restaurant and catering services, as well as commissaries also, in most such offices. Thus the scope for linguists is quite large. Translators, indeed, often go from one service to another if they so desire, or may be transferred from one agency to another, if they are interested in change of location.

Business firms with international interests also maintain in many cases their own translation staffs, with foreign correspondents for the export trade, as do many banks. Their staffs may be either permanent, or temporary for their conference work, which is considerable in the case of international groups such as the International Coffee Board, and others.

In some, but not all, the translator may also be called upon to do précis work, and a word about this may be in order. As we have seen, it is possible for a stenographer with a knowledge of languages to do précis work and ultimately translation also.

In the commercial concerns, précis may amount to little more than keeping the minutes of meetings, which may need to be reconciled in the end, however, with non-English-speaking delegates. Depending upon the scale of such concerns, the work may be detailed, or slight in extent; and it may or may not involve the use of tape recordings of proceedings. In the case of the international organizations cited, it is possible to provide more extensive information as to this little-known side of "translation" work.

Précis writing is carried out at meetings, as the word implies, for the purpose of summarizing proceedings and providing a record of what has been transacted. If a full report is required, this is called a verbatim record, and care must be taken, at times, to see that the exact words of statements are recorded. If the main proceedings only are needed, then the result is called a summary record.

Conferences held by the United Nations or under its auspices use various methods for the production of summary records. In most cases, meetings last for two and a half to three hours and teams of three English- and French-language précis writers draft the records of alternate meetings. The normal take is 50 minutes to 1 hour, and the record of each meeting must be written up by the end of the half-working day immediately following the meeting. However, records of afternoon meetings are written up the same evening in the case of the Economic and Social Council when it meets in Geneva and in that of the Law Commission, when that body holds afternoon meetings. The same is true of a number of other conferences held or organized by the Geneva office of the United Nations.

The Law Commission uses a system of its own, each meeting being serviced by two French and two English précis writers.

Certain U.N. technical bodies (for example, the Scientific and Technical Sub-Committee) draft minutes for the use of the Secretariat.

The organization of the main conferences of the I.A.E.A. is similar to that of the majority of U.N. conferences, with records of afternoon meetings being written up in the evening of the same day.

The W.H.O. also uses the standard U.N. system for sessions of the Assembly and the Board, records of afternoon meetings being drafted the same day. Meetings last from three to three and a half hours, and very full records are required. Records are always drafted in English and the précis writers—three per team —are provided with copies of the complete text of all speeches made in French and Spanish, and of the French interpretation of those made in Russian, typed from tape recordings. The document service is excellent, all the necessary documents being delivered to individual précis writers in their offices. At regional meetings, W.H.O. generally uses one form or another of the multilingual method.

The I.C.E.M. uses the same monolingual system, but with only two précis writers per team. Records of afternoon meetings must be drafted the same evening. Meetings are sometimes long, but the average duration of three hours is generally maintained.

The I.M.C.O. uses the same system, but does not as a rule employ more than two précis writers per team. Précis writers are required to dictate their records. Meetings last from two to three hours and records of afternoon meetings must be drafted the same evening.

The World Food Programme (W.F.P.) employs two précis writers per team and meetings can last up to four hours. Records, however, need not be full. The records of afternoon meetings are written up the same night.

Interpol also uses the monolingual system. Meetings vary in length and the work can be very heavy, but is paid accordingly.

Among nongovernmental organizations, the Union Interparlementaire allows half a day for writing up the records of meetings, which are shared by two précis writers and may last longer than three hours. For this organization, as for Interpol, records of afternoon meetings must be drafted the same evening.

The I.T.U. employs teams of two précis writers for records of meetings, which may last up to four hours. Afternoon meetings are written up the next day and précis writers seldom have less than a full day in which to complete their draft.

The I.C.A.O. normally uses précis writers only at headquarters, in Montreal. A single précis writer is required to write what is virtually an edited version of the verbatim record, for which he is allowed two and a half days.

The multilingual system, used by UNESCO, is more popular with delegations than with précis writers. Teams comprise one précis writer for each of the working languages, and reliefs are provided when any one language is likely to be used more than the rest during a meeting. Sometimes one member of the team, appointed *"chef d'équipe"* or *"coordinateur,"* is designated to organize the production and assembling of the final draft of the record; he is also held responsible for its accuracy. Records of afternoon meetings are written up the next day, and theoretically eight to twelve times the duration of the take is allowed for drafting.

The I.L.O. uses a variant of the multilingual system. Two précis writers, one French and one English, attend the whole meeting and divide the drafting of the record between them as they see fit. When records have to be produced in two or more languages, each of the précis writers may be required to translate his colleague's part. Records of afternoon meetings must be written up and translated the same night. Teams are composed of permanent staff seconded to conference duties, supplemented by temporary précis writers.

Perhaps the most striking general feature of précis-writing systems used by different organizations is their variety. Although the monolingual system is nearly universal, the chief exception being UNESCO, within that broad classification production methods vary in almost every respect.

Records range in length from the edited verbatim required by the I.C.A.O. to minutes used for purposes of the report by the I.A.E.A. at its technical conferences.

The time allowed précis writers for the drafting of their records is calculated in the United Nations on the assumption that it takes three and a half hours to write up the record of one hour of a normal meeting. The précis writer who has studied his documents and attended either the whole or part of a meeting (*i.e.*, long enough to cover his share of it with the necessary overlap at one or both ends and to have gathered the gist of the proceedings) is regarded as having done half a day's work and as needing the rest of the day to arrange his notes, check with recordings if necessary, and complete his draft. (In New York, précis writers must sit through the entire meeting.) In other words, attendance at a meeting and the completion of the draft record of one hour of the proceedings constitute a full day's work.

The practice of employing three précis writers per meeting has made headway in recent years but is still not accepted, or only partly accepted, by some organizations. Certain organizations, at their less important conferences, have asked three précis writers to cover two meetings a day between them. (Throughout one such conference, for want of a fourth précis writer, no records were made of the second half of the afternoon meetings.)

Systems and rates of pay also vary widely. Some bodies pay inclusive rates per hour of note-taking; in such cases, the tariff may range from $22 upward for the finished record of one hour of a meeting.

The Economic Commission for Africa (E.C.A.) uses the standard U.N. system with three précis writers per team, records of afternoon meetings being written up the following morning.

The 3½-to-1 ratio adopted by Administrations is a handy approximate criterion of the amount of time needed by the précis writer for the dictation of his draft record; but it must be carefully weighted if it is to be used as a basis for the calculation of the payment due to him. In particular, when records are drafted by a précis writer at home after a conference is over, special circumstances must be borne in mind. First, the précis writer may need to spend more time on work of this kind, not only because it will take him longer to arrange his notes, but also because the mere fact that he has notes of the whole conference before him will oblige him to edit his record. Second, he will need to arrange for or provide his own secretarial services; and third, his remuneration should include compensation equivalent to the paid weekends and public holidays enjoyed by his colleagues contracted by organizations as temporary staff. Payment made on an inclusive basis should likewise bear comparison with U.N. rates. For example, a précis writer who receives P.3 rates in the U.N. system should normally be paid at least $27.50 for one hour's completed record, plus an appropriate amount for secretarial services.

The number of précis writers per team is a question that can be decided only in the light of conference conditions in each case. Both the average duration and the scheduling of the meetings must be taken into consideration. When meetings are held regularly both morning and afternoon, the need for three précis writers per team is clearly greater than if meetings take place at irregular intervals, leaving as much as a day and a half or two days between them.

The multilingual system as applied by UNESCO is criticized on the ground that it is difficult, if not impossible, to ensure that work and the drafting time allowed for précis writers in the various languages is planned on a fair basis. The system could perhaps be modified along the lines of the I.L.O. method, combining it with the translation of records by précis writers into the various working languages, subject, of course, to the provision of adequate staff and time for the work involved. The advantage of some such arrangement would be that the précis writer who had less of the record to draft could have more of it to translate so that a fairer distribution of the work would be to some extent automatically obtained.

It is important to distinguish between records and minutes. Confusion can easily be created when secretariats ask for "only short records" or "more or less minutes," and as a result only a minimum number of précis writers is recruited. In the case of genuine records, the shorter the record the longer the time needed for drafting; only when minutes in the strict sense of the word are required can an economy in the number of précis or minutes writers be made.

A précis writer should be not only as quick as an interpreter in grasping the meaning of what is being said in a meeting, but also perhaps more certain of having grasped it correctly, since his version of the proceedings will be set down in black and white. This in turn calls for drafting ability more akin to that of the reviser than that of the translator. The qualifications represented by this combination of two high-grade skills could justify the grouping of précis writers in a category of their own, in the same way that interpreters have been grouped apart from the rest of language staff; and the paying of qualified précis writers at little short of interpreters' present rates.

When we think of the précis writer or translator sitting down before a tape recorder, listening to various speakers in a meeting, in order to produce a record of that meeting, we realize that we are living in a new era of communications. The translator is expected to be able to type efficiently, to take rapid notes, and to be able to operate a tape recorder with ease. So far he has not been called upon to operate a computer, or to do any computer programming, but the time is swiftly approaching when he will be expected to be as competent with computer equipment as he already is with the tape recorder.

Already the University of Brussels, at its Centre de Linguistique Automatique, has embarked on a project of a system of automatic dictionaries. This is communication at its best: instant retrieval, instant consultation, and the provision of more variants than can be given by an ordinary dictionary.

In the compilation of a machine dictionary the problem is to select an adequate number of words, of sufficient frequency, to provide coverage for the translation of new texts. Frequency counts of target-language equivalents are therefore required, but the problem of polysemia, or multiple meaning, is not thereby solved, and statistical investigation of language behavior must therefore be undertaken. In general it may be said that statistical criteria for evaluating the quality of automatic translation output still remain to be developed.

There are also possibilities of using automatic processes in such fields as indexing, information retrieval, and automatic abstracting, which cannot but prove most useful in translation and lexicological work.

For translators interested in mechanical languages, such as Fortran and others, there are great opportunities in the future, because these are actually "artificial" languages of a mathematical type.

In translation, as we have seen, however, meaning is the primary subject of interest. Relations between words are not considered for their own sake, as in structural linguistics, but are treated in terms of the function they have as *carriers* of meaning. Meaning is accorded a theoretical existence, and it is only by considering *content* as separate from form that we can say a passage in one language is a translation from a passage in another. Thus translation stresses both meaning and content. It is to be expected that these two elements, now rather neglected in linguistics and even art and literature, will before long regain the status they once possessed.

To produce a mechanical translation, a program must contain not only a dictionary but also an *algorithm*. The algorithm selects from the dictionary the equivalent required, and also carries out any rearrangement of the words of the translation. Machine translation is thus a part of the field of language-data processing.

The machine translation (M.T.) process falls into four stages: input, analysis of input-language units, synthesis of the output-language unit, and output. The first and last are mainly technological, whereas the two middle stages are the domain of the linguist. We might add a fifth, correction of the final text, the task of the translator. The program consists of a set of instructions given to the computer, and any large-scale computing machine can thus be transformed into a translating machine.

International Business Machines Corporation (I.B.M.) in this connection has built an internal storage unit large enough to hold an extremely large memory facility. This storage is a photoscopic disk, a serial unit read by optical techniques rather than magnetic sensing. The Rand Corporation on the other hand attempts to get the whole dictionary into the memory. Surprisingly good results have been achieved, and many difficulties have been overcome, but the outstanding one is the problem of semantics, or meaning, especially multiple meanings. Until semantic theory and research have progressed, the M.T. program can offer only alternative output sentences, or ambiguity.

The other problem is to decide how the dictionary is to be compiled, whether on the basis of grammar, or of roots. So far the question is unsettled. Clearly here, too, the translator has a part to play.

Much effort is being expended at present, in the United States, the Soviet Union, the United Kingdom, and Europe, on developing these techniques, especially for languages such as Russian and Chinese. Although there is no question of machines being used to replace the human translator, they may ultimately be used to cut down the volume of translation work and to upgrade human translators. This field requires knowledge of the apparatus and its uses and possibilities, as well as knowledge of linguistic analysis and semantics, and grammatical and translation experience.

With the development of electronic applications to lexicology, world centralization of terminology, in different languages, is only a matter of time. Many agencies are already working on this problem, among them the International Electrotechnical Commission in Geneva, which has a Technical Committee on Nomenclature; and, significantly, the International Union Against Cancer, which has a committee on nomenclature and statistics. This latter committee reveals how important translation and terminology can be in the fight against a universal scourge.

More generally, the Massachusetts Institute of Technology has for years been engaged in research work on the applications of technology to language studies, including machine translation.

As in other communications-engineering techniques, such as the telephone, linguistic signals are here translated into sequences of electric impulses, through a code system, and reconverted into written messages.

Speech is analyzed mechanically into its sound components by means of a sound spectrograph, once devised as an aid to the deaf. This produces a visual representation of the sound sequences. The use of such processes in interpreter training and advanced phonetics is clear, but their utility in communications generally is considerable.

Although the linguist is not directly involved in the mechanics of these and other techniques, he must be aware of what is going on in the various fields in order to be able to profit from them, and even assist in them, as does the translator who writes up or edits in acceptable language what translation machines produce.

This, of course, is primarily research work. The ordinary translator in the main field will have little to do with problems of this kind for a long time to come. As we have seen, he is the unaccountable "human" factor, too often ignored, whose total responses are much wider than anything mechanical, especially where "meaning" is concerned, or "terminology," which is not yet the domain of the machine.

A late news story will neatly sum up much of this chapter. It is reliably reported from Montreal, at the time of writing, that the International Radar Meteorology Conference at McGill University closed with bickering between scientists from the Soviet Union and other countries. What were they bickering about? Interference? Not a bit of it. The Soviet delegates complained that they had met a wall of "jargon" in the discussion and workshop sessions. Their interpreter apparently had a hard time translating what was said.

Dr. J. Stewart Marshall, Professor of Meteorology at McGill and organizer of the conference, admitted that terminology problems arose because many scientific groups were working in relatively new fields of study and sometimes evolved their own terms to describe their observations.

"We need to come to some sort of agreement on terminology," he said. When science inhibits communication, it is indeed high time that something be done along the lines suggested in this chapter. The problem is obscured by being regarded in isolation. It is common in all forms of communication through language, but especially in nuclear fusion and many other sciences. When will it be tackled properly? And by whom?

By you?

CHAPTER V

Related Fields and People in Them— "Anything That Talks"—Public Relations

There are possibly more fields related to translation work, both at home and abroad, than is the case with any other form of activity. We are using translation here, of course, in its widest sense, whether the translation carried out is the main activity or incidental to the main employment.

Many business concerns, we have already discovered, maintain a staff of translators or interpreters even in their home offices. These are now required for research purposes and to keep abreast of modern methods in the various branches of technology throughout the world; to translate abstracts dealing with new processes or discoveries; to peruse foreign technical journals and translate any relevant articles; to maintain a reference library and/or press-cutting bureau; or to accompany the managing director abroad on important negotiations.

Among firms maintaining branches abroad are large automobile manufacturers, with their assembly plants, sales and service, and depots for parts; the electronic industries; airplane engine manufacturers; fashion and food industries; and even English-language publications, one of which, in Amsterdam, translates thousands of articles every year, mainly in the field of medicine.

United States firms such as these have discovered in recent years that much business has been lost in Europe because of lack of familiarity with local methods, traditions, or psychology; not to mention ignorance of local tax regulations and customs, some of which are, to say the least, peculiar! This brings us to another important related field that is now opening up: public relations.

Public-relations work at home has, of course, long been recognized as vitally important. The phrase "public image" has passed into the language. In export areas, the public image is even more important and takes its place next to advertising in priority. Some of the largest concerns in the United States now operate their own public relations abroad instead of entrusting them to local representatives who may not be too well acquainted with American aims and techniques. In other words, American citizens are being increasingly selected for this field. It goes without saying that they are expected to be familiar with the languages and customs of the countries concerned.

The highest "public-relations" work is, of course, done by the State Department, and although the Foreign Service is not by any means restricted to translating work, here, too, knowledge of foreign languages and the ability to speak them is a necessary qualification. Much of the work in embassies and consulates does in fact involve translation, whether of commercial information, news items, or even, on occasion, legal material.

Similarly, travel agencies are in the habit of employing couriers, guides, and English-speaking personnel to staff their offices abroad; and airlines prefer stewardesses who are able to speak languages other than their own, though they themselves are citizens of the country operating the airline concerned. The language training for stewardesses is fully professional and adequate, as anyone will testify who has heard the charming feminine voices in aircraft, repeating instructions in two or three languages.

Fields related to translating and interpreting work, then, really cover "anything that talks." Telephone operators on the overseas services do a great deal of talking and are often expert linguists. So, too, are the many announcers on the foreign broadcasting and television circuits maintained at home and abroad by many governments.

One interesting though little-known form of employment is the "dubbing" of foreign films in English; or conversely, the dubbing of films of English origin in various other languages. This can be an art in itself, and it largely accounted for the enormous popularity of Laurel and Hardy films in Europe before World War II, especially in Italy.

In addition to the larger international agencies and commercial associations mentioned, such equally interesting organizations as the YMCA and YWCA are to be found all over the world; the International Red Cross; CARE; the World Council of Churches with its many ramifications; foreign missions, which have done invaluable linguistic work in little-known languages, including translation of the Bible into countless languages; the Travelers Aid Society; the United Seamen's Service; the prestigious Peace Corps; and other bodies too numerous to mention.

Much publicity has been given to the adverse side of the foreign policy of all countries, including that of the United States. In the absence of effective world government, this is only to be expected. Sensation is always news. Unfortunately the really constructive work done daily by these and other organizations is too often obscured, or taken for granted. This is a pity, but with time, it is bound to be realized, encouraged, and expanded. When this is the case, the image of the United States is bound to undergo a change, even at home, because, in a very profound sense, American society is a microcosm of world society.

It is therefore time that positive and constructive work be stressed. This is as much news as the "alarmist" type of information now so current, and it must be the task of responsible journalism. At least one highly successful monthly publication in the United States regularly prints articles from the press all over the world (including the Soviet Union), which are translated into English and published as they stand, without comment. It seems to me that with the world shrinking as it is, this is the type of journalism we must expect in the future; and, of course, it provides opportunities for translators.

Apart from this field, the glamorous "foreign correspondent," employed by leading press agencies, usually knows several languages also. In a high sense this, too, is public relations work.

Public relations has little to do with salesmanship—or has it? What a wall of sales resistance is constituted by an unknown language! The interpreter here becomes a skilled negotiator, because it is slowly being realized that the skilled negotiator is more often a man who knows and can handle language, or languages, as an instrument, than he is a psychologist. Few psychologists spend their time studying "foreign psychology" for business reasons. A word or two more about some of the above "public-relations" organizations may be in order. Although the U.S. Department of Labor does not, as far as I am aware, list translating or interpreting among its occupations, it must do so soon

RELATED FIELDS

PEACE CORPS

Peace Corps personnel on a colonization project in the Peten jungle of Guatemala.

because of the operation of the St. Lawrence Seaway, through which ships from European countries arrive directly at inland ports such as Chicago, Cleveland, and Detroit, thus expanding the need for the United Seamen's Service, with its interpreters and translators.

Travelers Aid, too, is expanding, owing to the daily arrival at airports throughout the country of nationals who in many cases speak no English.

At the growing number of ports and airports, customs and immigration officers who speak one or two languages besides their own are also required.

Hotels and resorts near airports or seaports are also drawn into the language side of the tourist business, which is growing by leaps and bounds, and are willing to pay premium salaries to employees with a knowledge of languages.

Surprisingly, interpreters are needed in larger hospitals and clinics; medical centers, too, are in need of translators fairly familiar with medical terminology. Interpreters' services have also long been required, sad to relate, in courts.

At home, employment for those with a knowledge of languages is also available with foreign embassies and consulates. Publicists, editors (for information sheets), stenographers, telephonists, and chauffeurs are all needed, but it should be remembered that those employed by foreign governments must register the fact with the U.S. authorities. In addition, every major department of government has its own library and information services, which employ language staffs to check the flood of reports and other information arriving daily from foreign countries. In Russian alone, for example, some 70,000 technical reports and professional publications enter the United States annually, dealing with such items as weather observations, Arctic conditions, drugs, surgery, space science, and rocketry. Everything must be translated; and the translator, if he is not a specialist or expert, must know where to find the relevant information.

Increasingly, as we have seen, such information is mechanically available.

Interpretation is equally in demand, however, as we realize when we think of the lengthy negotiations required in the matter of U.S. assistance to developing countries, an area in which the

United States often loses ground because it must employ non-American interpreters.

Finally, a little-known field related to phonetics is that of speech therapy. Speech therapists not only assist linguists, particularly interpreters, in pronunciation, but also aid English speakers to correct such forms of speech inhibition as stammering, or to correct any sort of accent that is too far removed from the standard. In the matter of voice production they may even be of assistance to actors and others concerned with public speaking.

Increasingly, the translator or interpreter who specializes steals the picture, as the man who knows what he is talking about. To "know what one is talking about" usually means to be able to express what one knows, or to interpret what has been said. It is a problem in translation, as well as an exercise in semantics. Surprisingly, however, too little attention has been paid to this aspect of language in business, except where "foreign" languages are concerned.

Other related fields abroad, besides foreign branches of national banks and companies, are the study of foreign markets, or market research, which can hardly be done without translation; the selection of trade representatives; and the work of such organizations as the National Foreign Council, or the Bureau of Foreign Commerce of the U.S. Department of Commerce.

There is also the possibility, especially in the United States, of joining one or other of the frequent anthropological expeditions to South America or elsewhere, and carrying out translation, interpretation, or research work among lesser-known Indian languages, now in the process of disappearing. It has been said that more can be learned about the life of early man from a study of such tongues as Eskimo or Cherokee than any amount of anthropological research will reveal, and today anthropologists are themselves interested in language as an aspect of culture.

Remembering that the language that is required may be your own, there is also a great deal of work available for translators and interpreters in the developing countries of Africa, such as Cameroon, Rwanda, Burundi, and so on. Many of these populations are French-speaking, and wish to learn English; or else English-speaking, and wish to learn French. There is thus the educational side to think of, as well as the purely translation field, although it is noteworthy that quite recently the Republic of Cameroon opened its first School of Translators.

Teaching has openings for language-laboratory supervisors, and language teachers in the countless Berlitz and similar direct-method schools abroad. These are mostly in private hands, but are to be found in most cities of any size. Work in them is always available. This, indeed, is a good way of seeing or residing in a foreign country to perfect one's knowledge of the language.

Systems of teacher exchange take place regularly between the United States and other countries, and as has been stated, the U.N. organizations frequently hold educational conferences in many countries, or engage those with a knowledge of languages in various fields on short- or long-term assignments.

"Anything that talks," indeed, is public relations also, and involves either interpretation or translation. Either of these accomplishments can therefore be a valuable adjunct to one's main interest, whatever that may be.

CHAPTER VI

Job Training and Where to Get It

Many universities are now alive to the need for proper translator training, which is often combined with general work in linguistics. Those qualified to train translators in their work are few and far between, however, and the linguistics scholar is apt to teach from a purely theoretical, and even "abstract," point of view, which for professional purposes is a pity.

The best courses, therefore, are those given within universities in so-called Schools of Translators, on the model of many such schools in Europe and Africa.* The best of these courses include a considerable amount of practical work, both from and into the native language. Although to some extent the study of linguistics may be regarded as a return of the bad old "grammar" lesson, it can teach valuable methods of quick translation from one language to another, largely by making us aware of our own linguistic processes. This is true especially of comparative linguistics and comparative stylistics, which compare and contrast two or more particular languages from the point of view of psychology, phrase structure, history, and so on.

After some twenty years of experience, however, in practice the translator will sit down to a new text as though it were his first, so much do linguistic problems vary in the task of interpreting one language to another.

In addition, such subjects as economics, political science, or international law should be made available, together with European or world history; at least one science and preferably two (mathematics and/or physics; engineering and/or biology); as

---

* The school in Geneva is famous. There are others in Paris, Ghent, Vienna, London, and recently, in the Republic of Cameroon, and elsewhere. One of the oldest is the Department of Language and Linguistics in Georgetown University, Washington, D.C.

well as one or two courses in linguistics, say semantics, the nature of language, and the theory of translation.

Existing language courses in universities are insufficient for translator training in spite of the growth of language laboratories, because they are of necessity concerned also with literature—indeed excessively with literature—and not enough with art and civilization in general. Nevertheless, they can be the nucleus of such training, especially if more attention is paid to the art of actual translation, an exercise that has fallen into disfavor in certain academic circles concerned with language teaching, as being too difficult, at least in undergraduate work.

Translators should be provided with the widest possible background, one that will enable them later on to concentrate, or specialize, in whichever direction they think fit, whether literary, technical, international, or commercial.

Training in machine-translation techniques can do no harm if it familiarizes the student to some extent with computer methods. Contrary to generally accepted opinion, however, translation is still an art. More precisely it has human content (language being a dynamic, living entity), which the machine cannot have. Should something resembling machine translation spread in the future, the machine is likely to produce a rough outline rather than a translation, thus requiring the services of translators for editing and revision. And I know countless translators who would much rather translate their own version than do any amount of what they regard as "fiddling" revision.

Time spent on this aspect would be much better spent, it seems to me, on including a science subject in the curriculum; or getting to know as much science as possible, not in order to master any science, but to become accustomed to scientific thinking and terminology.*

For technical translation, of course, technical knowledge is desirable, but it may be gained to some extent in practical work. Intelligently selected holiday jobs, tinkering with cars, and working in industrial plants are ways of acquiring the technical know-how no translator should be without.

Technical translation, naturally, is a field in itself, and this

---

* It is too much to look forward to a time when scientific research establishments will employ language consultants.

reduce output. It is astonishing how many private firms fail to provide this for their permanent translating staff, or to realize that it is uneconomical to have several people working in one small area.

Précis writers require the same working conditions as translators. A team of three members is needed to cover a normal three-hour meeting, and attendance at the meeting and the subsequent drafting of the record represent at least a full day's work for each of the précis writers concerned. If one meeting is held a day, one précis-writing team is required; if two meetings, two teams; and so on.

These conditions need emphasizing for the would-be summer, or temporary, conference translator or interpreter, who is likely to be unaware of the conditions he may face, but they also apply to the permanent staff, which at times is not very comfortably housed, and whose output therefore suffers both in quality and quantity.

It goes without saying that adequate dictionaries and documentation should be provided.

As to how to obtain such summer on-the-job training, the same advice applies as for getting jobs in general, as described in the next chapter. Ask for an application form for employment with the agency or company you have selected and send it in. You cannot complete too many of them! Then drop a line to the Chief Interpreter, Chief Translator, or better still "Head of the (English) Language Section" of the organization concerned, stating that you will be available for summer employment on a certain date and for a certain period.

The reason for this is that the Chief Interpreter or Chief Translator in many large organizations has a largely administrative job and rarely engages people himself. These are engaged by the Head of the English Language Section in international organizations, for example, whose duty it is to produce English versions of foreign-language documents and even journals. He is always interested in maintaining a list of potential employees; he will be glad to hear from you, and to arrange a test.

Be sure to let him know at what dates you will be free, so that he can consult his own timetable as regards conferences. And—as a form of insurance—do not be content to write to just one organization, but send out applications to at least half a dozen, and arrange to visit them when it is convenient. Your primary object is to get a foot in the door. Once you are known, other engagements will come of themselves.

A list of the universities and schools offering specific training in translation is provided in the Appendix to this book, but it should be realized that the list is not exhaustive. New schools open from time to time, and you should inquire at your local university whether any such school is contemplated, or available. If not, it may be that at least a course in some form of translation is available for undergraduate or graduate students. These should not be neglected.

On the other hand, the normal training for a B.A. degree in modern languages is adequate for the good student, and should suffice, if nothing else is available, as an introduction to the career we are discussing. Most teachers, at advanced levels at least, will be willing to include an extra bit of translation work in the course if they are asked. For this reason, universities offering outstanding tuition in modern languages are also listed in the Appendix.

In addition to vacation work at certain of the international agencies, useful on-the-job training is possible at various libraries and companies in the United States, even on a free-lance basis, or on contract.

The Kresge-Hooker Scientific Library of Wayne University, Detroit, Michigan, undertakes translations for corporations and research organizations, hospitals, and physicians. This translation work is directed by a professor who also edits a chemical journal, and the staff includes one full-time translator.

The Timken Roller Bearing Co., at Columbus, Ohio, prefers to use the services of free lances and translation bureaus for any translations it needs to have done, and there are many companies in this position, offering useful training to the aspiring translator.

The library of the U.S. Engineering Society in New York employs part-time translators, as do many other such libraries. In this way it is possible to build up a good connection of one's own. The Library of Congress, of course, also maintains a large

CHAPTER VII

How to Get a Job—Conditions to Expect— A Sample Contract

Depending upon whether you are interested in securing regular, permanent employment, or willing to undertake temporary appointments under contract, the procedure for obtaining results is slightly different.

Permanent appointments may be secured, if you are good enough, by taking the United Nations examination for translators and interpreters, which is given at irregular intervals in New York, Paris, London, and Geneva. The personnel officer of the United Nations in New York may be able to inform you of the date of the next examination; but it is best to watch the Appointments Vacant column of *The New York Times* or other large newspapers, in order to find out just when the examination will be given.

Meantime you will be well advised to ask for an application form in any case, and to complete it carefully in detail and send it in. One of the questions will be whether you are interested in accepting temporary employment. It is important here to say "yes," even if the idea does not appeal to you, and this for the following reasons, which are not understood by many candidates, or even explained by the powers that be.

The United Nations maintains two lists of candidates for employment who have taken the examination successfully. These are called A and B lists. The A list consists of candidates who have received the highest marks and are to be offered paid permanent employment at the first opportunity. These persons may be obliged to wait some time for an offer, but in the meantime they are given preference in any temporary vacancies arising out of special missions abroad, conferences, or other reasons. *All international agencies are obliged to accept such people when they are sent out from New York, or by the New York office,* to fill permanent or temporary vacancies, whether the agency concerned is the International Labor Organization, International Atomic Energy Agency, or another. Notice that I said "international" agencies. This ruling does not and cannot apply to intergovernmental agencies, such as the European Commission, Euratom, the Organization of American States, and so on.

The B list consists of candidates who, although not obtaining the highest marks in the examination, are of interest to the United Nations because of some of their qualifications; or because they are clearly qualified, but are unlikely to be offered immediate employment on a permanent basis owing to lack of vacan... It is important to realize that it is difficult to forecast such vaca... They may actually occur. For this reason it is useful to be on list B.

In the case of both A and B lists, however, temporary vacancies do occur in connection with missions and other duties. It may be inconvenient, or even impossible, for you to think of accepting such an offer. This is a mistake. Temporary vacancies are just as rare and important as permanent ones. In many cases, especially for those on the A list, they lead to permanent employment; or for B, to the useful post of "permanent" temporary, filling vacancies as they arise. So do not make the mistake of thinking that a "temporary" post is to be despised. It can be prolonged. And it is a first step.

While waiting for news of a possible permanent post you should apply for short-term work to gain experience. You will be granted an interview, and probably given a test for translators or an audition for interpreters. If successful, this will ensure free-lance work at fairly regular intervals, which is extremely remunerative and well worth while. Again, however, it should be noted that in the case of free-lance work of this kind, *each international agency is free to make whatever arrangements it likes.* Clearly, the New York office cannot be expected to know the day-to-day work or sudden needs of other agencies, so that such agencies are left free to offer short-term employment as they require, with the proviso that, if possible, A-list candidates should be preferred. In Europe, this is almost impracticable, except in the broadest sense. What this means, then, is that you should register your name for short-term work on the files of every international organization found in the *Yearbook of International Organizations* by writing to the personnel officer and asking for an application form. Even this is not enough, however; at the same time you should write to the Head of the English Translation Section, or whatever translation section is involved, telling him of your qualifications and experience, and informing him of the dates when you would be free for temporary work as translator, interpreter, or précis writer. If you can follow this up by a visit, so much the better. He will not regard you as a nuisance, unless you are overaggressive, but will be only too glad to have your name and address and to know that you are on call. Very often, heads of sections are in real trouble when it comes to temporary staffing, and they like to know well in advance who is likely to be available.

The same applies to intergovernmental and even nongovernmental organizations, scientific societies, and so on. They all have annual conferences or general meetings, and must find staff. Complete their application forms, if these exist, or write a letter explaining your interest, qualifications, and dates when free. The results will surprise you. Permanent employment may be the result, as many of these smaller bodies—also listed in the *Yearbook of International Organizations*—maintain skeleton staffs of translators. At the very least, you will add to your repertoire of temporary work if you are interested in free-lancing or running your own bureau.

Another way of obtaining employment is by joining one of the many associations of translators and interpreters. There is probably one in your area. These help to raise the standard of work done, and often carry out work for the government. Internationally, they include the International Federation of Translators (I.F.T.), the International Association of Conference Translators (A.I.T.C.), and the International Association of Conference Interpreters (A.I.I.C.), the last two with headquarters in Geneva. In New York, there is the Association of Professional Translators, which locates translation work for members and provides, free of charge, translators' aids published by the association; and also the American Translators' Association.

When applying to such organizations, include in your résumé, or curriculum vitae, details of your high-school or university record; languages spoken, written, and read, with degree of fluency (good, very good, or excellent); willingness to travel; starting salary; experience and any other qualifications, such as shorthand and typing; knowledge of office equipment, and so forth.

In Paris UNESCO also holds examinations for translators, in which the competition is extremely keen. It is said that 5 percent of candidates pass and 1 percent get jobs!

Besides the international and other agencies, export and import companies in your own area may be on the lookout for a translator or interpreter, and may provide useful experience. This is a good place to begin, either free-lance, or in a permanency. Pan American Airways, Trans World Airlines, and other air companies are also useful places to apply, as are the U.S. Chamber of Commerce (International Commerce Division); the American Management Association; transport companies with foreign freight departments; American Express, Thomas Cook, and other travel agencies or agents; the main shipping companies; large manufacturing companies, which probably maintain their own translation offices at home and abroad, such as the famous Batelle Memorial Institute, which has an office in Geneva; the American Institute for Foreign Trade, at Thunderbird Field, Phoenix, Arizona; and most U.S. consulates in the larger cities abroad. In view of the number of applications you may need to make in the course of time, it is advisable to have as many as fifty copies duplicated in advance.

The employment possibilities will depend upon your own interests outside of the translation field, and there are as many different opportunities as there are trades and professions. In the end, it is a good thing to specialize, if you can, though not necessary. Addresses of trade organizations are too numerous to be given here, or even in the Appendix, in full detail, but most may be gleaned from the public library.

For interpreters, it is well to note the increasing number of trade fairs of various kinds, and the enormous growth of the tourist industry, both of which engage interpreters well in advance. This is temporary work as a rule but, again, well paid and an excellent way of learning the ropes.

For those hardy souls who would rather work on their own, the opportunities are there. Setting up a bureau of one's own, or with a partner, with a pool of outside translators and interpreters to call upon, can net from $10,000 a year upward, especially in technical work, for which a pool of specialists can be formed. If this can be combined, as it is in many cases to my knowledge, with occasional trips to international conferences, life can become very pleasant indeed.

Conversely, be on the lookout for such private agencies in your own area, and have yourself inscribed on their pool of translators, but be careful. There *are* agencies, even today, that pay translators very badly, according to the bad old tradition when a translator was usually a new immigrant and, needing the money, was willing to work for very little. Standards were low, too, of course. Rates today are reasonable, and standards are much higher, so that you should not accept underpaid employment for any reason whatsoever.

Even in industry, there are still too many employers who will grant a translator the status of a prestigious "crank"; treat him with some abstract indulgence, like a bird of paradise at the zoo; and yet coop him up in a tiny office, with inadequate facilities in the way of library, references, or even documentation. These things should be asked for. It is well to remember that you are still a relative newcomer to the commercial scene, however, and therefore under inspection by all. Show that while you won't bite, you have no intention of being bitten, either!

In the all-important question of "status," the translator is in a peculiar position; yet if he knows how to behave, the work he does automatically qualifies him as a professional.

The conditions to expect in the field are therefore of necessity varied. You may be given a private office, but more probably you will work in an office with a colleague or even two others. You may be given the use of a secretary, but more probably you will have to share a stenographer's services with one or two others or use the typing pool. These conditions are largely outside your control. You will most likely be expected to type at least the first draft of your material, but you should not allow others to expect you to produce professionally typed copy. You are a translator, not a typist.

On the other hand, since noise and interruptions reduce output, you are entitled to expect peace and quiet and the opportunity to work undisturbed.

Payment is an important element. In general, in international agencies, you will start at the level of P-1 or P-2, with from $6,000 to $7,000 per year, and rise to P-3 and P-4 (reviser) and higher, with salaries of up to $20,000 or even more, depending on the range of duties and the responsibilities involved. These pay rates compare favorably with salaries in other fields in the United States, especially when it is remembered that permanent employees of U.N. organizations pay no income tax *of any kind,* and are often able to shop at bargain prices in private commissaries, free of sales tax or import duties. This considerably reduces the cost of such items as cigars and cigarettes, wine and liquor, and perfume or cosmetics!

These advantages are strictly for international personnel, however, including temporary staff. They should not be expected everywhere.

In commercial organizations, on the other hand, there are different advantages, such as representational allowances, which may be quite high. These are also payable in U.N. agencies, but only in the case of special missions abroad, whereas in business they are often granted whenever necessary, even at home.

In business, too, the use of a car, and various other discounts when shopping, often make up for the benefits accruing to U.N. employees, as do special facilities for importing various items.

In conclusion, it cannot perhaps be too strongly stressed that for the translator or interpreter it is important to think internationally, or "globally."

Mario Pei has written an interesting book called *Talking Your Way Around the World,* published by Harper & Row, and for an interpreter or translator this is actually possible. Jobs occur everywhere.

A friend of mine, Hamilton by name, for some time lived in Athens, Greece, with frequent trips to conferences in Vienna, or Rome, or even Geneva. He was a qualified engineer, with a knowledge of French and, I believe, some Spanish. Soon he had his "tour," as it was called, and visited these cities regularly for conference work, which for him included précis writing. He lived in Athens, he said, because he found it cheaper. His fare to the various conferences was, of course, paid by the agencies concerned.

Hamilton, however, was restless, and wanted to see more of the world. Following a few exploratory trips to Turkey and Persia, he took the plunge and attended a conference in Thailand.

His new headquarters became Bangkok. I am afraid his career there was not, strictly speaking, one of orthodox translation. Being a free lance and in an out-of-the-way area, he had to find employment in the interval between conferences, and he was not above selling alarm clocks in the mountains! However, as far as I know, he is happily settled there, and has traveled to Tokyo, Hong Kong, and Australia on conference work, in addition to the work he finds in Bangkok and India.

Another acquaintance has written of his experiences at a conference in New Delhi. Being eager to save as much as possible out of his "overseas" allowance (he was also saving the whole of his salary), he lived in hotels that were very modest indeed, and ate in Indian restaurants, where the food is ample and varied. As a result he came to know Indian life as few *"conférenciers"* do, and returned home with quite a large sum of money. He explained to me that he had to do this because he was altering and improving his home and needed large amounts of capital.

Conditions of work are thus as varied as one cares to make them. And the more one is prepared to travel, the more opportunities there are.

Some of the international scientific societies, for instance, also mentioned in the *Yearbook of International Organizations*, which hold regular annual or biennial conferences, are the International Cereal and Bread Congress, which met in Vienna in 1966; the International Society for Horticultural Science; and the International Tin Council.

By writing to such bodies and getting to know the dates of their annual, biennial, or even triennial conferences in advance, it is possible to make up your own program for two years in advance, and see something of the world into the bargain.

Apart from this, too, the national organizations themselves

have work to farm out among outside translators. Here the criterion is strict accuracy, since most of the material is technical or scientific. Many of these scientific societies have their own employment "clearing houses." The secretaries responsible will help you in each case.

Another source of employment, permanent or free-lance, is the columns of newspapers and trade and scientific journals, which more and more are advertising for translators.

The budding translator would do well, therefore, to make sure that his qualifications are registered not only in as many organizations as possible and with local or national associations, but also in such directories as the *International Directory of Translators,* published by the Pond Press in London.

To maintain fluency, there is nothing better than to make a practice of reading foreign newspapers. It is not necessary to look up every unknown word in the dictionary, which can be discouraging. Often the meaning can be guessed. When you have read awhile, certain words will emerge as of fairly frequent occurrence. Look up these. Gradually you will find there is less to look up.

It is useful, too, to keep a small notebook for vocabulary, but be careful about this. Many students fall into a trance-like state in which they write down everything, with the feeling that once it is written down, they know it. Nothing could be further from the truth. Psychologically it is a comfort, that is all.

The notebook must be read and reread, conned at every spare moment. If the foreign word is in the left-hand column, and the English on the right, it is useful at times to cover the English with your hand and see if you remember the meaning of the foreign word. *Conversely,* learn to cover the foreign word and see if you can find the foreign expression for the English one. This will make you realize that there are two forms of vocabulary, the vocabulary you can recognize and the vocabulary you can use, or the passive and active vocabularies.

Although the translator may find he concentrates on the passive vocabulary, and that it is enough for him to recognize a word at sight, the interpreter must necessarily be able to *use* his words. He will therefore have to cultivate his *active* vocabulary, by finding the proper phrase for these on the English side of his notebook.

There are also periodicals that make a point of printing the same stories and anecdotes simultaneously in several languages. Buy these and use them too for your own purpose, for noting down new words and phrases, idioms, and colloquial expressions. You will notice that the "translation" is not always word-for-word, and sometimes may not even be very good. This, however, serves to bring out the great difference conveyed in the *mental picture* provided by the various languages.

These exercises will keep your knowledge of the various languages fresh and up-to-date in your mind, and facilitate fluency in speech, as well as strengthening and expanding your vocabulary.

A SAMPLE CONTRACT

(for international agencies)

LETTER OF APPOINTMENT

To: Mr., Mrs., Miss ....
.... (full address)
From: ....
      (Name and address of employer)

We are pleased to offer you an appointment from ....
to .... as reviser, précis writer, translator, editor.

1. *Place of work:* ....
   You are requested to report for duty on
                        (date and time) ....
   at (address) ....
   to Mr., Mrs., Miss ....
   who shall be responsible for liaison between the language services and the organizers.

2. You will be required to*

   —*translate* from .... into ....

   —*revise* translations from .... into ....

   —*edit* documents in ....

   —*write, revise** summary records of meetings for which the working languages will be ....
   Simultaneous, consecutive* interpretation will be provided in ...., will not be provided.*

   You will have the secretarial assistance required to enable you to complete the summary records or translations within the time limits set by common agreement.

3. *Remuneration*   (*In U.S. dollars*)

You will receive ...... dollars (or the equivalent in convertible and transferable currency) per day, including Saturdays, Sundays, and holidays, for the duration of your engagement, that is, a total sum of ....

4. *Traveling expenses and subsistence allowance*[1]

You shall also receive:

   —an amount corresponding to the cost of a first-class return ticket for travel by air,[2] rail, or boat, with a single cabin or sleeper for travel by night, that is: ..

   —the cost of airport taxes and transport between the aerodrome and the center of the city on arrival and on departure, that is: ....

---

* Please cross out the words which do not apply.

[1] Applicable only to translators employed elsewhere than at their professional domicile.

[2] Tourist class may be accepted providing the translator is allowed 30 kg of free luggage. Please find attached herewith an order which will enable you to transport an additional 10 kg free of charge or an amount representing the cost thereof both ways, that is . . . dollars.

— an amount equivalent to 50 percent of the daily remuneration for the day before the beginning and the day after the end of the appointment, that is: . .

— a daily subsistence allowance (per diem) of . . . . . . dollars for each day of absence (whether a full day or a part of a day) from your place of domicile, that is, for . . . . days' absence: . . . .

— a lump sum for incidental expenses, which shall be not less than 12 dollars, that is: . . . .

— the following additional allowances:

For travel by air you shall be entitled to:

— one day's rest with salary and per diem for journey of more than 9 hours and less than 16 hours;

— two days' rest with salary and per diem for journeys of more than 16 hours and less than 21 hours;

— three days' rest with salary and per diem for journeys of 21 hours or more;[1]

that is, ... days at . . . . . . dollars per day for the return journey: . . . .

TOTAL

5. *Cancellation of Contract*

In case of cancellation of contract you shall be paid the following compensation:

a) 50 percent of the agreed basic salary for the whole period of the appointment if the contract is canceled more than 30 days before the beginning of the appointment;

b) 100 percent of the agreed basic salary
   (i) for the whole period of the appointment if the contract canceled within 30 days of the beginning of the appointment;

---

[1] Rest days may be taken during a stop en route or on arrival.

(ii) for the period of the appointment to run if the contract is canceled during the appointment;

c) subsistence allowance (per diem) for a minimum of three days in addition to the salary due under paragraph b) above if the contract is canceled during the appointment.

6. *Hours of work**

The length of the working week shall not exceed 40 hours, spread over 5 or 6 days. It shall not exceed 35 hours if you have to be on duty after 8 P.M. (evening shifts), or 30 hours if you remain on duty after midnight (night shifts).

If, owing to unforeseen circumstances, you are called on to work longer than the normal hours specified in the foregoing paragraph, you shall receive compensation in the form either of time off, or of an equivalent number of days of paid leave on termination of the contract.

The number of supplementary hours worked shall not exceed 8 per week for day shifts, 7 per week for evening shifts, and 6 per week for night shifts.

7. *Method of Payment*

a) The subsistence allowance (per diem) shall be paid on your arrival, for a period of two weeks or for the period of your appointment, and thereafter every two weeks, in advance;

b) your salary shall be paid every two weeks;

c) all sums due to you, whether in respect of salary, subsistence allowance, or travel expenses, shall be paid at least 48 hours before the end of your appointment;

d) all sums specified in paragraph c) above are tax free;

e) your salary shall be paid, at your choice, in dollars or convertible currency, either by bank transfer or by check made out in your name. These amounts shall be immediately transferable to your country of domicile.

---

* In regions where the climate is such as to make working conditions especially difficult, the appropriate adjustments shall be made to the hours of work.

8. You are asked kindly to return one signed copy of this letter of appointment to us as soon as possible.

9. Kindly inform us:

a) which of the methods of payment specified in paragraph 7 e) you prefer;

b) whether you wish us to send your ticket;

c) whether you wish to have a hotel room reserved for you.

```
..........,  ......... 19..           ...............................
 (Place)       (Date)                  (Signature of employer)
```

I hereby accept the appointment described in this letter, subject to the conditions therein specified.

```
..........,  ......... 19..           ...............................
 (Place)       (Date)                  (Signature of translator)
```

CHAPTER VIII

*Job Satisfaction—Some Perquisites—
Travel—Salaries and Allowances*

The one great source of job satisfaction in translating or interpreting work is its infinite variety of theme, scene, and companionship. One never knows what to expect. Each translation presents a new problem and a new topic. Travel—to Africa, India, Europe, America—is as frequent as one wishes, and sometimes too much so. Friends and colleagues change, but are always somewhere to be found.

There is also the satisfaction of the work; of having done something to further human understanding, however little. And a "built-in" cultural background, since one has another literature to read, and sometimes more; another world to look at; music and opera by the best performers, often permanently available.

The financial rewards, if not as considerable as in some sections of business, are fairly high, and at times, especially abroad, free of income tax (U.N. employees pay none). Living abroad and receiving U.S. salary is the quickest way to save money.

There is also less competition abroad from one's own fellow countrymen. The United Nations, for example, has a quota system for employment, and not too many Americans, and very few Canadians, are there in any capacity.

Plenty of opportunities for advancement exist in one's own field, where authority is easily established after a few years; or in kindred fields, such as editing and publishing, and publicity in general.

There is a sense of creativity throughout, and the pleasure of working harmoniously with colleagues comparatively free of pressure of any kind; in other words, quite a lot of independence.

It is often possible, for instance, to transfer to another organization without difficulty. One acquaintance went from the

International Telecommunication Union to the South Pacific Commission in New Caledonia for two years, and returned to the International Labor Organization in Geneva. International civil servants are permanently established, with tenure, making this possible; but large-scale companies at times offer still more in the way of travel abroad and "expenses."

I cannot imagine a finer or more interesting life than that of translator or interpreter living and working in foreign countries and helping to establish a feeling of international community and real kinship with all peoples.

The commissaries run by various international bodies have already been mentioned. There one may buy everything from groceries to clothing, at prices much lower than those in any country, since there is no duty or sales tax to pay. Such agencies also have well-run libraries and reading facilities and one or two excellent restaurants or cafeterias, where the food is plentiful, well cooked and inexpensive, and not restricted to local dishes.

There are local markets to visit, art galleries, and musical concerts, which often include opera performances of world standard. This applies particularly, of course, to such leading cities as New York, Washington, London, Paris, Geneva, Rome, or Vienna.

On the various relief missions to the East, or to Africa, there are also places of interest that few but world travelers ever have an opportunity to see at their leisure, from the Pyramids of Egypt to the Taj Mahal in India and the game parks of Africa.

This, in fact, constitutes the greatest "perquisite" of all, the ability to travel practically wherever you wish if you have the patience to wait for the right opportunity. I have known translators stationed in Vienna to fly on a brief mission to Mexico; others stationed in Geneva to fly to Tokyo, or exchange with people in New Caledonia; and free lances in Europe or New York to visit Africa (including Burundi, Kenya, Ethiopia, the Congo, and Morocco) as I have done, or Bombay and New Delhi, as others have done. This is probably the greatest attraction in the career of translator, at the top level, and it does help to produce a world consciousness.

In business, too, especially for interpreters working in North America, travel to Central or South America, and Europe as well, is a frequent possibility.

The Peace Corps in the United States has its employees in the field all over the world, doing linguistic work that is both pioneering in nature and heroic in character.

The experience and memories gained from such trips remain throughout life. If combined with some skill in photography, they can be a never-ending source of delight and wonder to friends, relatives, and acquaintances, not to mention grandchildren, as well as a deep source of satisfaction because of the knowledge they bring of the treasures as well as the tasks of mankind.

"All right," you may say, "but what has all this glamour to do with me? I shall probably be working in the same place and at the same job all my life."

To this I would retort: "Do not be too sure! In that one place, and one job, you will acquire skills that can perhaps be acquired nowhere else, and will cause your services to be in demand in quite a number of other places!" Say you are engaged mostly in translating, for a technical firm, data on chemical processes in industry. This will possibly also involve translating abstracts from chemical journals from time to time, insofar as they affect the techniques of your firm. New processes will be discovered or frequently discussed that may involve your corresponding with, or visiting, countries in any part of the globe; applications will arise that may be of interest to UNESCO and involve attending a conference; and the same may be true with certain safety precautions, about which you will be expected to report to your local industrial safety officer, and perhaps to the C.I.S. in Geneva. No one, in fact, lives in a world of isolation any more. We all live in the same world, and all that goes on in it is our concern.

After such lofty thoughts, it is, I admit, something of a comedown to have to discuss such mundane things as salaries. The phrase "It's only money" is an apt comment on the steadily decreasing part that money plays in our lives as compared with what are now called "fringe benefits."

We have already discussed some fringe benefits. In permanent employment, health insurance and hospitalization are covered in many cases, although the real riches come from the knowledge of the world we have been discussing. Actual salaries in the U.N. and other organizations have been mentioned. There is no reason to assume that in business they are any less, but this, of

CHAPTER IX

Health and Security—Retirement and Pension—Currency and Other Hints

From the point of view of health and security in our troubled world, there would at first sight appear to be some drawbacks to the career of translator and interpreter, whether in the United Nations or elsewhere. This applies particularly to climate.

Africa, however, is no longer the "White Man's Grave." The advance of modern medicine has meant that one can live there in comparative comfort, even in areas once regarded as unhealthful. True, there is still sleeping sickness in parts of the coast; malaria exists, although pills twice a week take care of that; and other tropical diseases have not been entirely conquered. Yet on the whole there is little more discomfort today living in Africa than in living at home. The same applies to such out-of-the-way places as Indonesia or Malaysia. Any lack of amenities is more than compensated for by the magnificent flora and fruits.

Such areas, however, are the exceptions. Generally, following a short period of adjustment to foreign climate and food, the translator settles down happily enough, wherever he is.

No locality, of course, is ideal. For some, the atmospheric pressure in Geneva, with its rapid changes, is a source of annoyance. For others, the heat and lack of movement in the air of Vienna in summer is hard to bear. There is the winter in Moscow; the fog in London; the drought in New York. But all these are comparatively minor discomforts, which are more than made up for by the various pleasures these cities have to offer.

In this connection, I am reliably informed that in spite of antimalaria pills, one does get a mild form of malaria in parts of Africa, which persists and is recurrent, though the effects amount to nothing much worse than a slight cold and a feeling of depression. Inoculations against the various tropical diseases, such as smallpox, yellow fever, cholera, and so on, are required before embarking on any of the missions described to tropical countries. These can have misery-producing effects, but recovery ensues in a day or so.

The free lance should subscribe to some form of health insurance in order to avoid sudden, large medical bills, although as long as he is working for an organization he will probably be covered, both with respect to hospitalization and accidents.

Those who are in permanent employment should remember that theirs is a sedentary occupation, with its attendant disorders, in time, of circulatory and heart troubles. They should ensure that they get enough exercise at weekends—by playing golf, skiing, swimming, or merely walking—and not carry on in their leisure hours as they do in the office, perusing books and fatiguing their minds.

Free lances are not so subject to the dangers of a sedentary occupation, since they get about more, have a frequent change of scene even when they work at home, and are, so to speak, their own bosses.

Here lies a different type of danger, and an insidious one. I refer to the danger of stress. When you are working for yourself, there is always the temptation to overwork and overstrain. This should be resisted. All translators and interpreters are expected at times to work very long hours indeed. At various conferences I have worked all night at times, and although this is uncommon, to get away at midnight when working on a shift at a conference is indeed a favor to be appreciated. If, in addition to this, you happen to be a free lance working at one conference after another, the dangers become clear. One is working then all the time at top speed and full-out, whereas the permanent employee can at least retire to his office and await another conference at a later date, sometimes not for a year.

The free lance, tempted by the high salary and additional allowances, accepts one contract after another and is tempted to cut out vacations, since he does not and cannot know when he may fall idle for a spell. In practice he may well find himself working constantly, without a break, not unlike a doctor on call, over a period of some years. This is the worst possible form of stress from the medical point of view and, I repeat, should be firmly resisted. It is not often that one comes across the type of very kind Head of Section who says, as one said to me, "We are offering you another three months' contract on one condition . . . that you take a two-weeks' holiday, at our expense, in the mountains."

In fairness, however, I ought to say that to some extent even for free lances, there is a built-in guarantee against ill health—the fact that for long-term contracts, and often for short ones, a medical examination is compulsory. Never have I undergone so many medical examinations, or X rays, as when working as a free-lance translator. Since these were all free of charge, and doctors prescribe a regular checkup in any case for everyone, this really constitutes another "fringe benefit" and health safeguard.

Nevertheless, the threat of undue stress always persists, especially when the Head of Section—like one I prefer not to name—overworks his staff unnecessarily to the point of breakdown.

Much the best way of avoiding this is to take regular holidays and get a real change of scene and air. The permanent employee takes care to do this. The free lance must discipline himself to do so and to take up some form of energetic sport, for which he is bound to have ample opportunity.

In the matter of social security, the international civil servant, as has already been pointed out, loses nothing, and even gains in having no income tax to pay.

The situation is not the same for intergovernmental employees, the employees of private firms, or even those of international associations. In these cases, the employees retain their social security rights, even when working abroad, but are also subject to national, but not local, income tax.

If the firm concerned is small, however, or a local one abroad, the difficult question of a work permit may crop up. Most countries today require nonnationals of a state to have work permits before they may take employment. Normally the employer will arrange this. In the case of such organizations as Berlitz Schools or private translators there should be no difficulty—and no permit may even be required—because the employment concerned is not such that it could be carried out by a native. Nevertheless, such countries as Switzerland make matters extremely difficult. To avoid "overheating" the economy, a drastic reduction was recently made in the number of foreign workers employed, and no one was allowed to work in the country unless he or she already had a contract of work and a work permit.

A few anecdotes will reveal the circumstances that still obtain. A friend, offered a post by an international organization, was lucky enough to find a small apartment in the center of Geneva at an exorbitant rent. A few days later he was interviewed at home by a member of the Swiss police delegated to "domestic" police duties. He was politely informed that the purpose of the visit was to discover the amount of rent he was paying, as there was a law against excessive rents. Later he was asked when he had arrived in Switzerland; where he was employed; whether he had a residence permit(!) or a work permit; and how long he intended to stay, this being a rather vicious way, it seems, in Europe, of making visitors for any length of time feel unwelcome. Our friend was able to satisfy the policeman on one count at least. He worked for an international organization, he said, naming it.

In a few days, the policeman was back with the statement that at the said organization nobody appeared to know him. Clearly the purpose of the visit was not the rent after all. The gentleman concerned pointed out that they could not be expected to know him as he had only just arrived. Matters were left there.

A residence permit can be a serious business. An American woman, living in the Alps in her own villa at about the same time, was also politely asked by a local gendarme why she was living in Switzerland at all. She replied that the villa was her own, and that she wanted to be near her daughter, who was at a Swiss school in the neighborhood. To her astonishment, she was then asked:

"Well, Madame, do you think that really is sufficient reason for making your residence in Switzerland?"

So if you should think of visiting Switzerland, that beautiful country, be sure to have a contract before you set out and obtain residence and work permits as soon as you arrive. Most international organizations now issue a form of identity card bearing your photograph, if you are employed by them.

And one final word. *Should* you be lucky enough to obtain a post in that country, open a Swiss bank account. Swiss banking services are the finest in the world. And *keep* an account there, even after you leave. It will come in useful for all sorts of things, including holidays. Switzerland is still the financial clearing-house of the world.

It is only in the matter of pensions that free lances at present are in some difficulty. The Association Internationale des Traducteurs de Conférence is at present endeavoring to set up a system of pensions in agreement with the large organizations, but so far nothing has been achieved. This is a disadvantage that may be offset to some extent by the fact that in translation work there is no real retiring age. An old gentleman of my acquaintance retired officially on reaching the age of seventy, but still regularly translates for that perennial source of delight for translators and interpreters alike—the Disarmament Conference.

So far we have not mentioned this Olympian body. Few people, probably, are aware that it exists. It may cheer them up considerably to know that a permanent Disarmament Conference is in session regularly in Geneva, attempting to reach agreement on the final scrapping of all weapons. Neither the East nor the West dares risk the plunge in prestige that would follow a breakdown in negotiations by either side, so they keep up the interminable talks. And, of course, translators and interpreters are required, on a standby basis. Could anything be more wonderful? At least for translators and interpreters?

And when, or if, agreement is reached some day, there will still be a flood of reports, proposals, suggestions, and counter-suggestions to be translated, leading no doubt to the setting up of still another international organization—complete with translators and interpreters, permanent and temporary—to supervise the actual carrying out of disarmament over a 25-year period, and report back annually, until the end of the century! Well, talking is always better than fighting. Some say talking has even become fighting. All the more reason then, surely, to learn how to fight-talk.

The old gentleman I mentioned is happy to work at his disarmament, as in a worthy cause. He has retired, after all.

The currency in which one is paid, of course, is a matter to which some attention should be given.

The Swiss franc is a universal currency, as are U.S. and Canadian dollars; but some countries, including the United Kingdom, place a limit on the amount of local currency that may be taken out of the country. Care must be taken, therefore, to see that there is no limit set on the free flow of your money, by insisting either in payment in a freely convertible currency, or on a free transfer of funds. Some of the African countries, perhaps through inexperience, have been rather remiss in this regard, and expect translators to travel out on the promise of a contract at the other end. This should be frowned upon. It is rather too late, once you have arrived in Africa, to start discussing whether the contract is acceptable! Especially when the only alternative to accepting it, bad as it may be, is to pay your own way home!

It is also as well to make sure about such matters as baggage allowance, what you are allowed to take in and out in the way of purchases, and so on. There can be extremely stiff rates for air excess baggage. Some countries, too, ban the export of antiques that may interest you. If you happen to be on a U.N. Mission, the possession of a U.N. passport may be of assistance, but do not rely on it; always carry your own national passport in case of emergencies, whether or not you are working on after retirement!

One of the final advantages of working as a translator begins to emerge only at the end of one's career, and at the end of this description of the career—and that is mobility.

Mobility of labor has always been recognized as advantageous to the person selling his labor. In the uncertain world of today, mobility—the ability, even physically, to live anywhere, given the opportunity—is an asset that it is hard to overestimate and difficult either to control or do without. I would not like to think it was one of the last of our freedoms.

CHAPTER X

*How to Make a Self-Evaluation—
Opportunities for Women—The Best
of Careers*

Any student of languages realizes before long whether he is gifted in the field, whether he likes writing in English, whether he appreciates style in his own language, and whether he likes to tackle the problem of transferring the style of a piece of prose in another language into his own. As these realizations dawn upon him, what he is doing in fact is making a self-evaluation. Strange to relate, in the end, he is the only one really capable of making an evaluation of his own suitability. Examinations are no real test of ability, subject as they are to good or bad luck, off days, badly phrased questions, and so on. They test something of what one knows, or rather does not know: the amount one knows and understands is rarely evaluated properly.

When it comes to the actual merit of the translations a student does, however, true self-evaluation is difficult. There are excellent books on the market, in the *Teach Yourself* series, for instance, that facilitate home study. Others, such as the Ritchie and Moore *French Composition,* provide students with passages for translation both into and out of French, for the purpose of self-testing; and at the same time furnish sample model translations, enabling a keen student to try to bring his standard up to professional level.

Students should be warned that this is a difficult job, and one requiring a great deal of practice, patience, and study of style. A large vocabulary is needed in both languages, together with a sense of the genius, or semantic relations in each language. Do not despair. Translation is an art, remember, and demands above all great sensitivity to language, your own and the foreign one. Only constant practice can achieve this.

These textbooks are at a fairly high level, and there is little in between to help the student attain that level, or to give him an adequate possibility of estimating his own potentialities.

One good method of doing this is to make translations regularly of parts of foreign newspapers that interest you. Such a translation should be as good and as idiomatic as you can possibly make it. When it is completed, leave it for a day or so, and then try to translate it back into the source language. Compare your effort with the original version. The results will shock and alarm you, but do not be too depressed. You will rarely be expected to write as well as a native speaker. That is the most difficult thing in the world to do, yet such efforts are the best possible way of self-evaluation.

When you begin to take a little pride in the English of your foreign version, you are making progress. As they say, "you have it in you."

The other, almost automatic, way of conducting a self-evaluation, of course, is by taking examinations. Apart from university and college examinations, qualifying examinations are given by the various translators' associations for admission to membership, and you can be fairly sure that when you have passed one of these, you at least have a foot on a rung of the ladder. Many firms will also give you a short test when you apply for a job. These should all be grist to your mill, as providing further proof of the progress you have made.

Many publishers also issue books in bilingual editions. Harrap has a series of classics, with the original on one page and an English translation on the other. Here again is an excellent way of testing your ability to translate novels. Cover the English page with a book, and try to produce your own version. It does not matter how many dictionaries you consult, or how long you take; the point is to compare your own version in the end with the printed one. In time you will be surprised to find how little difference there is, apart from questions of style.

Again, international organizations constantly put out literature in all five official languages of the United Nations. This is a way of widening your vocabulary and of taking short tests along the lines of those set by U.N. agencies.

Unfortunately it is difficult, if not impossible, to obtain copies of U.N. or UNESCO examination papers. These are not published. Why this should be so, I do not know. To be admitted to the examination, one must have a university degree, so competition is keen. At the end of the examination, papers must be handed in. Apparently there is strict control over these. The only solution, then, is to take the examination purely to test yourself and see the standard required. The standard is very high, and mistakes entail automatic failure. It should be mentioned also that failure in French results in failure in the examination as a whole, which to me constitutes quite unjustified weighting in favor of French. It means that a brilliant Russian scholar whose French is weak has no chance, a ludicrous state of affairs for an international organization, and one we must hope will soon be remedied.

I do not think it will be regarded as a revelation of state secrets to say that the examination consists of texts for translation into English, which are drawn from various sources. There is usually a general one, from French, involved in style, and requiring careful drafting in English; a scientific one, from physics, medicine, or nuclear science; an essay in French; and similar texts for translation from Spanish, Russian, and so on, depending on the languages one offers. These may include Italian and German. By training in the translations of such texts, therefore, you will be able to test whether you have a chance of passing the examination at a sufficiently high level.

As regards interpretation, conditions are more specialized. Every modern language department at college or university is equipped these days with an up-to-date language laboratory, which are nominally open to students in their spare time. There they may hear their own versions of translations or interpretations, as recorded by themselves. It is relatively simple, therefore, for a student to cultivate and test his own abilities in either simultaneous or consecutive interpretation, with the help of a colleague or professor; one student, or the professor, reading a text over the intercom in English or in French, and those inter-

Students at work in a linguaphone class at the 1st Moscow State Pedagogical Institute of Foreign Languages, U.N. Language Training Center, Moscow.

ested interpreting it into their own language or into the foreign language, as the case may be. As this interpretation is recorded on tape, it can be played back and checked at will. It can be translated later onto paper, and discussed in class.

The United Nations maintains a training section that uses such methods, and one of these is in Moscow. It is comforting to know that training can go on, even when one has obtained a post!

It will be seen, then, that self-evaluation in the case of translation is something that goes on all the time.

When you are traveling abroad it is fun to try and pass as a native of the country and see how far you can get. Only on rare occasions will you actually pass. More often you will be given any nationality but your own, but even this is a consolation, since you have at least avoided easy identification!

Private translating agencies, finally, will be glad to allow you to do sample translations for them, which will provide an objective judgment of your abilities.

The field of translation and interpretation, like the field of language teaching, includes perhaps a larger proportion of women than do most other professions. This may be a follow-through from the teaching world, but it should be said that women appear to be particularly well suited to act as interpreters. They possess the necessary gift of empathy, to begin with; and, of course, are more attractive to look at and listen to than the average male! Thus they establish a rapport with an audience. If they cultivate an out-of-the-way language such as Russian, their future would seem assured, and yet, certain intangible elements enter in: reactions may not be quick enough; the voice may be unsuitable, or indistinct; or there may be an inability to remember or to summon up technical phrases readily enough. In any case, I have known women, apparently ideally gifted, who have failed to pass the tests. The same, of course, applies to men. Although there are many women translators, I wonder whether they are really happy at this sedentary occupation, in which they do not occupy the center of the stage; or, shall we say, to be tactful, in which they are not allowed to demonstrate their natural love of activity?

A male translator of my acquaintance, who was a bachelor,

maintained that all women are aggressive. As an instance, he cited their stiletto heels! I have not found this to be so, but I have a feeling that interpretation or précis work are perhaps better expressions of the female temperament.

Be that as it may, women in this field have perhaps greater opportunities than men:

a) because more of them take up language study;
b) because they are naturally interested in helping people and in establishing a rapport;
c) because they are active, and "extrovert" in most cases; and
d) because so many of them train as stenographers that they dominate the field of précis writing, which, as stated, is a stepping-stone to translation work, if that is the goal.

Needless to say, no prejudice against women is to be found in the profession. The bachelor mentioned above was peculiar in his views, and indeed was regarded as eccentric by his colleagues.

As an instance of the growing opportunities for women in the profession, I should like to quote the example of a woman who regularly appeared at various conferences throughout Europe as a précis writer and minute writer and now trains women staff members for UNESCO conferences.

Women interpreters or translators are also in particular demand as guides, air stewardesses, receptionists, telephonists, telephone operators, hospital interpreters, secretaries, and so on. They are extremely adaptable, and many of them are skilled at both précis and translation work and can turn their hand to either. That their basic skill is précis writing merely means that their translation is perhaps slightly less professional. That does not matter. They did not claim it was outstanding. In this field it is important to state what you can do well, and what you are less good at. You will be called upon to do everything in time, in any case. But modesty creates confidence. Perhaps here, too, the feminine element scores.

Everything considered then—salary, possibilities of travel, independence of movement, and mobility, not to mention the cultural aspects of the profession—I think it would be hard to find any occupation more delightful, and less boring, than that of translator or interpreter, whether one is permanently employed by a private firm, bureau, government, or international agency, or whether one is working on one's own. Why the profession should not be too well known has always been a puzzle to me; and yet, as I have said, it is an individual and independent occupation, and those actually engaged in it are much too busy and happy to take time out to write about it.

This is also perhaps why the nature and technique of translation has been so neglected, too, in linguistic studies, another promising field for the translator. The good translator, like the good medical man or scientist, would rather practice than preach. So go to it—and with my blessing on all your difficulties and endeavors.

APPENDIX A

Universities and Colleges Offering Degrees in Translation or Courses in Linguistics, With or Without Translation

Most U.S. and Canadian universities have a fairly full curriculum in modern languages, including French, Spanish, German, Russian, and in some cases even Chinese. The number offering degrees in translation as such is smaller but steadily growing. The following are a few of those where linguistics, often including translation, is taught, as well as the above languages.

UNITED STATES

University of Arizona, Tucson
Boston University, Massachusetts (the Department of Modern Languages organizes professional courses in French translation)
Brooklyn College, New York, N.Y.
Brown University, Providence, Rhode Island
Bryn Mawr College, Bryn Mawr, Pennsylvania
University of Southern California, Los Angeles 7, California. (School of International Relations, with Bachelor of Foreign Service degree)
University of Chicago, Illinois
The City College of the City University of New York, New York
Columbia University, New York City. The Writing Division of the School of the Arts, 440 West 110th Street, New York, N.Y. 10025, announces a two-year program in writing, leading to the Master of Fine Arts (M.F.A.) degree. Within the framework of this program a Translation Seminar is planned, and visiting writers and translators will lecture.
University of Connecticut, Storrs
Cornell University, Ithaca, New York
University of Delaware, Newark

UNIVERSITIES AND COLLEGES OFFERING DEGREES

Duke University, Durham, North Carolina
Georgetown University, Washington, D.C. (the School of Languages and Linguistics has a celebrated Translation and Interpretation Division)
George Washington University, Washington, D.C.
Harvard University, Cambridge, Massachusetts
Indiana University, Bloomington (offers course in translation in Department of Linguistics)
Institute of Foreign Studies, Monterey, California (School of International Conference Interpreters opened in 1966)
University of Kansas, Lawrence
University of Louisiana
University of Louisville, Kentucky
Massachusetts Institute of Technology, Cambridge (pioneers in machine translation)
University of Michigan, Ann Arbor
University of Minnesota, Minneapolis
New York University, 3 Washington Square N., New York, N.Y. 10003 (Translation Seminars in French, German, and Spanish)
Ohio University, Athens (a Workshop in Translation set up in the Department of English in 1967, for the purpose of encouraging literary translation work)
University of Pennsylvania, Philadelphia
Rutgers—The State University, New Brunswick, New Jersey (trains Peace Corps volunteers in many languages)
University of Texas, Austin
University of Vermont, Burlington (provides translation courses in French, German, and Spanish)
University of Washington, Seattle (Graduate Seminar conducted on The Art of Translation, within the Program on Comparative Literature)
University of Wisconsin, Madison
Yale University, New Haven, Connecticut

CANADA

University of British Columbia, Vancouver
Carleton University, Ottawa, Ontario (offers a course in translation as part of degree in French)

Laurentian University, Sudbury, Ontario (offers four-year course in translation, which includes three languages, and also political science, economics, linguistics, and sciences, with rigorous translation training from assorted texts; Interpreter's Diploma awarded after extra year; degree of Bachelor of Science in Language)

McGill University, Montreal, Quebec (issues diplomas and certificates in translation through the Department of Extension)

University of Montreal, Quebec (offers arts degree in English and French translation; produces the excellent *Meta* journal of Translation, showing the work being done in Canada on problems of terminology)

University of Ottawa, Ontario (offers a course in translation as part of the Master of Arts degree in linguistics, theoretical in approach, confined to English and French; no technical translation undertaken)

Simon Fraser University, Burnaby, British Columbia

UNITED KINGDOM

Battersea Technical College, London

University of Bradford (offers full translator's course, with practical work and summer employment in Europe)

University of Salford, Department of Modern Languages (Offers a broad course in Linguistics)

University of Wolverhampton (Three-year course leads to degree in European Languages and Institutions)

BELGIUM

University of Brussels (Centre Linguistique, problems of terminology and machine translation)

University of Ghent (School of Translators)

University of Mons, School of Translators and Interpreters

CZECHOSLOVAKIA

Faculty of Social Sciences, Prague University, Translation and Interpretation Department

FRANCE

University of Paris (School of Translators)

UNIVERSITIES AND COLLEGES OFFERING DEGREES

GERMANY
Dolmetscher Institut Johann Gutenberg, University of Mainz, Germersheim
University of Heidelberg (School of Translators)

ITALY
Università degli Studii, Scuola d'Interprete, Trieste
Università degli Studii, Istituto di Lingue Straniere, Rome

SWITZERLAND
University of Geneva (École d'Interprètes)

APPENDIX B

Publications and Specialized Dictionaries

French, Monolingual

Dictionnaire Quillet de la langue française, Librairie A. Quillet, Paris, 1959, 1961.
Mon Premier Dictionnaire français, Philip Linklater, University of London Press, London, 1961.
Dictionnaire de la langue française, Emile Littré, Editions Universitaires, Paris, 1958.
Dictionnaire de l'Académie Française, Firmin-Didot, Paris, 1878.
Dictionnaire générale de la langue française, A. Hatzfeld, Delagrave, Paris, 1900.
Langage et Traduction, Pierre Daviault, Bureau Fédéral de la Traduction, Sécretariat d'Etat, Ottawa.

French, Interlingual

The Concise Oxford French Dictionary, Abel Chevalley, Clarendon Press, Oxford, 1934.
French and English Dictionary, J. E. Mansion, Harrap, London, 1939.*

Spanish, Interlingual

Cassell's Spanish Dictionary (Spanish-English, English-Spanish), Funk and Wagnall's, New York, 1960.
Appleton's Revised English-Spanish Dictionary, Arturo Cuyas, Appleton-Century-Crofts, New York, 1953.
The University of Chicago Spanish Dictionary, University of Chicago Press, 1948.
New Revised Velazquez Spanish and English Dictionary, Mariano Velazquez de la Cadena, Follett Publishing Co., Chicago, 1961.

---

* Refers to outstandingly useful works.

PUBLICATIONS AND SPECIALIZED DICTIONARIES

German, Interlingual

Brockhaus Illustrated German-English, English-German Dictionary, McGraw-Hill, New York, 1960.
Cassell's German-English, English-German Dictionary, Harold T. Betteridge, Funk and Wagnall's, New York, 1958.*
Harrap's Standard German and English Dictionary, revised ed., Harrap, London.
The New Wildhagen German-English, English-German Dictionary, Karl Wildhagen, Follett Publishing Co., Chicago, 1965.
Langenscheidt's Enzyklopädisches, Wörterbuch der englischen und deutschen Sprache, Langenscheidt, Berlin-Schöneberg, 1962.

Italian, Interlingual

Cassell's Italian-English, English-Italian Dictionary, Cassell, London, 1958.
Dizionario inglese-italiano, italiano-inglese, Michele Ciaramella, Vallardi Editore, Rome, 1966.
A Short Italian Dictionary, Alfred Hoare, Cambridge University Press, 1964.
The Follett's Zanacelli Italian Dictionary, Giuseppe Ragazzini, Follett Publishing Co., Chicago, 1968.

Italian, Monolingual

Il Novissimi Melzi, dizionario italiano in due parti: linguistica, scientifica, Gian Battista Melzi, A. Vallardi, Milan, 1951.

Russian, Interlingual

New English-Russian, Russian-English Dictionary, M. O'Brien, Diver Publications, New York, 1944.
New Complete Russian-English Dictionary, Louis Segal, Praeger, New York, 1959.
Russko-Angliiskii Slovar, Aleksandr Ivanovich Smirnitski, E. P. Dutton, New York, 1959.*
Anglo-Russkii Frazeologicheskii Slovar, Aleksandr Vladimirovich Kunin, Moscow, 1967.

Russian, Monolingual

Tolkovyi slovar zhivogo velikorusskogo iazika, Vladimir Ivanovich Dal', Moscow, 1955.

Portuguese, Interlingual

The New Appleton Dictionary of the English and Portuguese Languages, Appleton-Century-Crofts, 1967.

Brockhaus Portuguese-English, English-Portuguese Picture Dictionary, Novo Michaelis, Edicões Melhoramentos, São Paulo, 1958.

Dutch, Interlingual

Cassell's Dutch-English, English-Dutch Dictionary, Dr. F. P. H. Prick Van Wely, Funk and Wagnall's, New York.

Swedish, Interlingual

Svensk-engelsk ordbok skolupplaga, Walter Ernst Harlock, Svenska Bokforlaget, P. A. Nordstedt & Soner, Stockholm, 1964.

Japanese, Interlingual

Japanese-English, English-Japanese Character Dictionary, Andrew N. Nelson, Charles E. Tuttle Co., Rutland, Vermont, 1966.

Chinese, Interlingual

Concise Chinese-English Dictionary, James C. Quo, Charles E. Tuttle Co., Rutland, Vermont, 1966.

Concise English-Chinese Dictionary, James C. Quo, Charles E. Tuttle Co., Rutland, Vermont, 1966

Technical Dictionaries (various languages)

General

Spanish and English Technical Dictionary, Castilla, Routledge and Kegan Paul, London, 1958.

Ketteridge's Technical Dictionary, English-French, French-English, Routledge and Kegan Paul, London, 1959.

Chamber's Technical Dictionary in English, Chamber's, Edinburgh.

*Chamber's Engineering Dictionary.**

Glossary of Terms Used in Electrical Engineering, British Standards Institution.

PUBLICATIONS AND SPECIALIZED DICTIONARIES 119

Glossary of Terms Used in Telecommunication, BS204, British Standards Institution.
Glossary of Terms Relating to Automatic Digital Computers, British Standards Institution.
International Meteorological Dictionary, World Meterological Organization, Geneva.
An International Electrotechnical Dictionary, I.E.C., Geneva.*
List of Definitions of Essential Telecommunication Terms, I.T.U., Geneva.
Dictionary of Structural Mechanics and Related Fields, in 5 languages, Z. Bazant.
Dictionnaire Technique des Barrages (French, English, German, Spanish, Italian, Portuguese), International Commission on Large Dams, World Power Conference.
Russian-English Technical Dictionary, L. Callaham.*
Russian-English, English-Russian Telecommunications Dictionary, Department of the Army, Washington, D.C.*
Russian-English Dictionary of Automation Terms, A. V. Khram.
Russian-English Dictionary of Guided Missile, Rocket and Satellite Terms, A. Rosenberg.
Elsevier's Automobile Dictionary (Wörterbuch) in Eight Languages.
Elsevier's Rubber Dictionary in 10 Languages, Rubber Foundation, Delft.
French-English, English-French Electronics, C. G. King, Dunod, Paris.*
Chamber's Diccionario Tecnologico (Spanish-English, English-Spanish).
French-English Science Dictionary (Agriculture, Biology, Physical Science), I. De Vries.*
Hoyer-Kreuter Technical Dictionary, French-German-English.
Glossary of Work Study Terms, O.E.E.C., Paris.

Mathematics

Russian-English Mathematical Dictionary, L. M. Milne-Thomson, CBE, University of Wisconsin Press, Madison, 1962.
Russian-English Mathematical Vocabulary, J. Burlak, Oliver & Boyd, Edinburgh, 1963.

Mathematics Dictionary (English, French, Russian, Spanish, German), R. G. James.
German-English Mathematical Vocabulary, S. MacIntyre and E. Witte.

Electronics

English-Russian, Russian-English Electronics Dictionary, McGraw-Hill for the Department of the Army, Washington, D.C.
International Electrotechnical Vocabulary, Group 20, I.E.C. Geneva, 1958.
Russian-English Glossary of Electronics and Physics, Consultants' Bureau, New York.
French-English, English-French Electronics, C. G. King, Dunod, Paris.*
Dictionnaire electronique français-anglais, C. G. King, Dunod, Paris.

Nuclear Physics

Seven Language Nuclear Dictionary, D. I. Voskoboinik, Moscow, 1961.*
United Nations Atomic Glossary (French, English, Spanish, Russian), United Nations, 1958 (in process of revision).
Russian-English Atomic Dictionary, E. A. Carpovich.

Chemistry

German-English Dictionary for Chemists, A. M. Paterson, Wiley and Sons, New York.*
Russian-English Technical and Chemical Dictionary, L. I. Callaham, John Wiley and Sons, New York, 1960.
French-English Chemical Dictionary, A. M. Paterson, Wiley and Sons, New York.*
The Van Nostrand's Chemist's Dictionary, J. M. Honig, M. B. Jacob, S. Z. Lewin, et al.
Diccionario de Quimica (Spanish-English, English-Spanish), A. and E. Rose.

Geology

Diccionario Minero, Metalurgico, Geologico, Mineralogico, Petrografico, etc. (English, French, Spanish, German, Russian), Alexander Novitzky, Buenos Aires, 1960.*

PUBLICATIONS AND SPECIALIZED DICTIONARIES 121

Concise International Dictionary of Mechanics and Geology,
S. A. Cooper.
Polyglot Dictionary of Mineral Species, O. E. Nakhimzhan, Moscow, 1962.

Medicine

Russian-English Medical Dictionary, Stanley Jablonski, ed. B. S. Levine, Academic Press, New York, 1958.
Merck Index of Chemicals and Drugs, Merck and Co., 1952.*
Blakiston's New Gould Medical Dictionary, Hoerr, Osol Editors.*
Russian-English Biological and Medical Dictionary, E. A. Carpovich.
Dictionnaire Français-Anglais et Anglais-Français des Termes Médicaux, P. Lépine.

Other Reference Books

Manuel de l'Interprète, J. Herbert, Georg, Geneva, 1952.*
Conference Terminology, Herbert, Glossaria Interpretum, Hilversum, Holland.*
Dictionary of Commercial, Financial and Legal Terms, R. Herbst.
The Complete Dictionary of Abbreviations, R. J. Schwartz.
Webster's Dictionary of the English Language.*
The Oxford Dictionary.
Van Nostrand's Encyclopedia.*
Engineering Handbooks (various, including Nuclear).*
Acronyms Dictionary, Gale Research Co., New York, 1960.
The English Duden, Der Grosse Duden, Duden Français, pictorial dictionaries, Bibliographisches Institut, Mannheim Germany, Abt. Dudenverlag.
La Traduction dans le Monde Moderne, E. Cary, Georg, Geneva, 1956.

APPENDIX C

Reading List

Aitken, Thomas, *A Foreign Policy for American Business*, Harper & Row, New York.

Alekseev, M., *Problema xudozestvennogo perevoda* (The Problem of Artistic Translation), Sbornik Trudov Irkutskogo Gos., Universiteta 18, 1931.

Amos, F. R., *Early Theories of Translation*, Columbia University Press, New York, 1920.

Anderson, H. H. and G. L., eds., *An Introduction to Projective Techniques and Other Devices for Understanding the Dynamics of Human Behaviour*, Prentice-Hall, New York, 1951.

Arrowsmith, William and Shattuck, Roger, eds., *The Craft and Context of Translation*, University of Texas Press, Austin, 1961.

Axelrod and Bigelow, *Resources of Language and Area Studies*, American Council on Education, Washington, D.C., 1962.

Bally, Charles, *Le Langage et la Vie*, Editions Atar, Geneva, 1913.

Bloomfield, Leonard, *A Set of Postulates for the Science of Language*, 1926.

———, *Language*, Holt, New York.

Boas, Franz, *Race, Language and Culture*, Macmillan, New York, 1940.

Boulding, K. E., *The Image*, University of Michigan Press, Ann Arbor, 1956.

Brower, Reuben A., ed., *On Translation*, Harvard University Press, Cambridge, 1959.

Carnap, Rudolf, *The Logical Syntax of Language*, Kegan Paul, Trench, Trubner & Co., London, 1937.

———, *Meaning and Necessity*, University of Chicago Press, Chicago, 1947.

READING LIST

———, *Logical Foundations of Probability,* University of Chicago Press, Chicago, 1950.
Cassirer, Ernst, *An Essay on Man: An Introduction to a Philosophy of Human Culture,* Yale University Press, New Haven, 1944.
———, *Language and Myth,* Dover Publications, New York, 1946.
———, *The Philosophy of Symbolic Forms,* Vol. I, Yale University Press, New Haven, 1953.
J. C. Catford, *A Linguistic Theory of Translation,* Oxford University Press, London.
Chomsky, Noam, "Syntax and Semantics," *Syntactic Structures,* pp. 92–105, Mouton, 's-Gravenhage, 1957.
Church, J., *Language and the Discovery of Reality,* Random House, New York, 1961.
Croce, Benedetto, *Aesthetic—as Science of Expression and General Linguistic* (trans. D. Ainslie), Macmillan, London, 1929.
Crystal, D., *What Is Linguistics?,* Arnold, London, 1968.
Entwhistle, William J., *Aspects of Language,* Faber & Faber, London, 1953.
Gordon and Washburn, *New Horizons in Education,* P.A.A., New York, 1961.
Gentilhomme, Y., *A Manual of Russian for Scientists* (trans. J. F. Hendry), Dunod, Paris.
Graff, W. L., *Language and Languages: An Introduction to Linguistics,* Appleton, New York, 1932.
Greenberg, Joseph H., *Essays in Linguistics,* University of Chicago Press, Chicago, 1957.
Hayakawa, S. I., ed., *Language, Meaning and Maturity,* Harper, New York, 1954.
Hockett, Charles F., *A Course in Modern Linguistics,* Macmillan, New York, 1958.
Hogben, *Interglossa,* Penguin Books, 1943.
Jakobson, Roman, Fant, C.G.M., and Halle, Morris, *Preliminaries to Speech Analysis: The Distinctive Features and Their Correlates,* Acoustics Laboratory, Massachusetts Institute of Technology, Cambridge, 1952.
Jespersen, Otto, *Language: Its Nature, Development, and Origin,* Allen & Unwin, London; Holt, New York, 1922.

Korzybski, Alfred, *Science and Sanity: An Introduction to Non-Aristotelian Systems and General Semantics,* International Non-Aristotelian Library Publishing Co., Lakeville, Conn., 1948 (Science Press Printing Co., Lancaster, Pa., 1933).

Kronasser, Heinz, *Handbuch der Semasiologie—kurze Einführung in die Geschichte, Problematik und Terminologie der Bedeutungslehre,* Carl Winter, Heidelbert, 1952.

Lévy-Bruhl, Lucien, *Les Carnets de Lucien Lévy-Bruhl* (preface by Maurice Leenhardt), Presses Universitaires de France, Paris, 1949.

Morris, Charles W., "Foundations of the Theory of Signs," *International Encyclopedia of Unified Science* I.63–75, University of Chicago Press, 1938.

———, *Signs, Language and Behavior,* Prentice-Hall, New York, 1946.

Parker, W. R., *The National Interest and Foreign Languages,* National Commission for UNESCO, New York; and U.S. State Department, Washington, D.C.

Pei, Mario, *The Story of Language,* Lippincott, New York, 1949.

Nida, Eugene, *Towards a Science of Translating,* E. J. Brill, Leiden, 1964.

Postgate, J. P., *Translation and Translations,* Bell, London, 1922.

Potter, Simeon, *Modern Linguistics,* André Deutsch, London, 1957.

Ritchie, Richard L. Graeme, *A New Manual of French Composition.* Cambridge University Press, Cambridge.

R. H. Robins, *A Short History of Linguistics,* Longmans, Green and Co., London.

Sapir, Edward, Language: *An Introduction to the Study of Speech,* Harcourt, Brace, New York, 1939.

Saussure, Ferdinand de, *Course in General Linguistics* (trans. by Wade Basking from *Cours de linguistique génerale,* Payot, Paris, 1916), Philosophical Library, New York, 1959.

Savory, Theodore H., *The Language of Science,* André Deutsch, 1953.

———, *The Art of Translation,* Jonathan Cape, London, 1957.

Sebeok, Thomas A., ed., *Style in Language* (Technology Press, Massachusetts Institute of Technology, Cambridge), Wiley, New York, 1960.

READING LIST

Turbayne, Colin Murray, *The Myth of Metaphor,* Yale University Press, New Haven, 1962.
Ullman, Stephen, *The Principles of Semantics: A Linguistic Approach to Meaning,* 2d ed., rev., Jackson, Glasgow; Blackwell, Oxford.
UNESCO, *Report on Scientific and Technical Translation,* Paris, 1957.
Vinay, Jean-Paul, *Stylistique Comparée du Français et de l'Anglais,* Harrap.
Weinreich, Uriel, *Languages in Contact,* Linguistic Circle of New York, 1953.
White, Leslie A., *The Science of Culture,* Farrar, Straus, New York, 1949.
Whorf, Benjamin Lee, *Language, Thought and Reality; Selected Writings,* John B. Carroll, ed. (Technology Press, Massachusetts Institute of Technology, Cambridge), Wiley, New York, 1956.
Wiener, Norbert. *The Human Use of Human Beings; Cybernetics and Society,* Houghton Mifflin, New York, 1954.
Wright, Arthur F., ed., *Studies in Chinese Thought,* University of Chicago Press, Chicago, 1953.
Wright, Neil, *Teach Yourself to Study,* E.U.P.
Ziff, Paul, *Semantic Analysis,* Cornell University Press, Ithaca, N.Y., 1960.

APPENDIX D

Professional and Other Societies

American Translators' Association, P.O. Box 489, Madison Square Station, New York, N.Y. 10010 (publishes "The American Translator").
The Institute of Linguists, 91 Newington Causeway, London, S.E. 1. England. (Publishes "The Incorporated Linguist.")
Association of Professional Translators, 258 Broadway, Room R729, New York, N.Y. 10007
The Association of Translators and Interpreters of Ontario, Suite 207, 371 Gilmour Street, Ottawa, Ontario
Société des Traducteurs du Québec, Inc., Quebec
Corporation des Traducteurs professionels du Québec, Montreal
Association Internationale de Traducteurs de Conférence (A.I.T.C.), Geneva, Switzerland
U.S. State Department, Washington, D.C. (for translation assignments)
Translation Bureau, Department of State, Ottawa, Ontario (for translation assignments)
The European Translation Centre, 101 Doelenstr., Delft, the Netherlands
Union of International Associations, 1 rue aux Laines, Brussels, Belgium
The International Directory of Translators and Interpreters, Pond Press, 46 St. Augustine's Avenue, Ealing, London W.5, England
D. F. Long and Co. (Translations) Ltd., 68 Newington Causeway, London S.E.1, England (for Language Consultants' Group, with offices in Benelux, France, Italy, and Germany)
The International Committee for Breaking the Language Barrier, Midtown International Centre, 268 West 12th Street, New York, N.Y. 10014

PROFESSIONAL AND OTHER SOCIETIES 127

International Coffee Board; International Olive Oil Association; International Rubber Council; International Sugar Council; International Tea Council; International Tin Council; International Cereal Association, and many others (see *Yearbook of International Organizations* for dates of annual meetings and translation requirements)

The American Council on Education, 1785 Massachusetts Avenue, N.W., Washington, D.C. 20006 (for information on study programs and teaching)

Consultants' Group (Pergamon Institute), 122 East 55th Street, New York, N.Y. 10022 (for publication of Russian journals relating to atomic energy, electrotechnics, physics of metals, and microbiology; also translation work)

The Institute for International Education, 800 Second Avenue, New York, N.Y. 10012 (for information on international universities)

Swiss Technics (published in a five-language edition by the Swiss Office for Trade Development, Zurich, Switzerland)

World Fisheries Abstracts (in four languages, published by the Food and Agriculture Organization (F.A.O.), in Rome, Italy

The Special Libraries Association, 30 East Tenth Street, New York, N.Y. 10003 (publishes a translation monthly, and records translations)

The Office of Technical Devices, Department of Commerce, Washington, D.C. (publishes a guide to Russian scientific periodicals, with a card index of translations.

New York Life Insurance Company, 51 Madison Avenue, New York, N.Y. 10010 (for pamphlets on career possibilities)

APPENDIX E

Interested Firms and Institutions That Are in the Profession

The following firms and institutions in North America have manifested their interest in the profession by maintaining a Sustaining, Corporate, or Institutional Membership in the American Translators Association, P.O. Box 489, Madison Square Station, New York, N.Y. 10010.

Sustaining

Bertrand Studio, New York, New York

Corporate

Addis Translation International, Woodside, California
Fifth Avenue Translation Bureau Ltd., New York, New York
Foreign Language Center, South Orange, New Jersey
International Translators, New York, New York
Scientia-Factum, Inc., New York, New York
The Christian Science Publishing Society, Boston, Massachusetts
The Language Service, Inc., New York, New York
Translation Services, Inc., New York, New York

Institutional

University of Toronto Library, Toronto, Ontario

CENTRAL PIEDMONT COMMUNITY COLLEGE

3 000564280